D1479393

SO-ANN-635

HEY, I'M MARTY. I DRIVE THE BUS! BOOK II

If you have ever driven a bus or
have been a passenger on a bus;
you must read this book!

MARTIN MOLINARO

authorHOUSE®

AuthorHouse™
1663 Liberty Drive
Bloomington, IN 47403
www.authorhouse.com
Phone: 1-800-839-8640

Photographer Rose Molinaro

© 2010 Martin Molinaro. All rights reserved.

No part of this book may be reproduced, stored in a retrieval system, or
transmitted by any means without the written permission of the author.

First published by AuthorHouse   9/22/2010

ISBN: 978-1-4520-6370-6 (e)
ISBN: 978-1-4520-6368-3 (sc)
ISBN: 978-1-4520-6369-0 (hc)

Library of Congress Control Number: 2010912748

Printed in the United States of America

This book is printed on acid-free paper.

Because of the dynamic nature of the Internet, any Web addresses or links contained in
this book may have changed since publication and may no longer be valid. The views
expressed in this work are solely those of the author and do not necessarily reflect the
views of the publisher, and the publisher hereby disclaims any responsibility for them.

DEDICATION

To my boys: Bob, Marty and Bill. Life is not always fair. Get over it! Be careful out there and no BS!!!

Dad

INTRODUCTION

Driving a bus is like the weather because you never know what tomorrow is going to bring. The people who ride the bus are as predictable with their actions as the Weather Forecasters are with the weather. It's a hit or miss situation. I'm not trying to ridicule anyone; all I'm trying to do is figure out why people do what they do. Now, that in itself is a rather large under taking, so; I'm going to have to take it one step at a time. Before I start to ponder and try to come to any conclusions; I need to set my goal parameters and try to figure out what I'm trying to figure out. Did I lose you yet? Let me try to explain.

I drive a city transit bus in a moderately sized city and I come in contact with many people. These people are from all walks of life; each and every one of them has their own story. First and foremost what I need to realize is that I don't need to know everything about my Passengers. I drive the bus! All I need to know is how I'm going to tell their story through my observations to you. Does that make sense to you? I think I just answered my own question!!

People ride the bus for many reasons. Most of those reasons are out of necessity. Whatever the reason is, Transit Systems are becoming more and more utilized by the general public. I venture to say that the rising cost of gasoline probably is the biggest reason for the influx of new bus riders.

Some not so informed people think; that just because you ride a bus that there is something wrong with you. I don't believe that for a minute! Hey I'm on a bus everyday and actually look forward to being there.

People that make negative comments or comments in general about bus riders are not too informed and don't know what they're missing. When you're on a bus, you're in a different world. A society within our society, I might say.

My perspective is a little different from the Passengers because the Passengers are only on the bus for a short time. The Passengers get on the bus and when the bus gets to their destination they get off the bus. I would say that most of the time what they're witnessing is only a portion of the stories that are being played out by the other bus Passengers. It's like the Passenger comes on the bus in the middle of the conversation that the other Passengers are having and the Passenger that just boards the bus never gets a chance to witness the entire story that is being played out. It is not that confusing if you think about it.

That's where I come in. I'm here to tell you their stories and to probably fill them in on what they missed. I may at times go overboard and gives to much information. Get over it, that's just me and I'm telling the stories. I tell many people that when they are reading my stories; that it is not a good idea to be drinking a glass of milk at the same time. I'll give you a second or two to think about that one. It's not that I'm judging people, I'm just the middleman in the entire picture and I'm trying to relay to you their actions through my thoughts.

Everybody has a story to tell regardless what they do for a living. Some stories are just more interesting than others. I think that its how the story is told is what makes the difference. I'm sure that if a Mathematician or Mortician would tell me one of their work stories that they thought to be hilarious; the story would only be funny to me only after they explained it. You see when people tell stories about what they think is funny, it is only funny if they tell the story so that others can understand it. One should not use topic jargon or words that nobody understands when telling a story. The only time jargon should be used is if the people that you're talking to are familiar with the topic.

Enough of that lets get down to business. Just for fun the next time that you are a Passenger on a bus or a shuttle ask the Driver if he or she has ever driven with no hands on the steering wheel. I'm sure that they will give you a bizarre look. No, really they will. Or perhaps they will tell you that it's unsafe and that they would never do anything like that. Then after you have them thinking; ask the Driver how he or she closes the door with their right hand; turns on the turn signal with their left hand and at the same time merges the bus or shuttle into traffic? See where I'm going here? If both hands are doing something different, how are they driving with no hands on the steering wheel? Are they steering with their knees?

I've looked in all the Department of Transportations rules and I can't find anywhere in the rules where it's O.K. to drive with no hands on the steering wheel and the use of your knees to steer. This is true with semi tractor trailers too. How do they shift gears put their turn signal on and switch lanes at the same time? I'm sure that those that do it have no idea that they're doing it. And if they do it they wouldn't admit it anyways. I thought that I'd give you some food for thought. I like doing that because it keeps people on their toes.

When someone is operating a bus or shuttle, their best friends are their two side mirrors. The rearview mirror is usually useless most of the time, unless the Driver wants to scan the interior of the vehicle. The interior mirrors most of the time won't help scan the outside the vehicle. If the side mirrors are use properly they can save the vehicle operator a lot of frustration. First for the mirrors, to be effective, they must be adjusted so that they are being used properly. I have to laugh when I see a person driving a bus and they try to back up as if they're driving a car. What they do that cracks me up is that they turn their heads to the right and look over their right shoulder as if they're backing up a car. Heck all they're going to see are Passengers look back at them. Then, it's really funny the way that they hold their right arm up as if it's resting on a seat. That's an accident waiting to happen.

If it can be avoided buses and shuttle should not be backed up because there are too many blind spots and the chances of the Driver hitting something increases ten fold. If a Bus Driver uses his mirror effectively, they will know what is around the bus and should avoid any accidents. Knowing their height clearance is just as important as knowing their side clearances. It doesn't do any good to know one area is safe and not the other. Common sense comes in play here and quite a few times it isn't used.

Steering the bus can be hard work if the Driver tries to wrestle with the steering wheel. It also is not very ergonomically wise either. Carpal tunnel and numerous shoulder injuries can occur if the Driver steers the bus the wrong way. Repetitive motion is the culprit here. Aside from having their seat properly adjusted their driving techniques need to be adjusted to prevent injuries. Next time you're on a bus check out how the Driver steers the bus. If the Driver turns the steering wheel with one hand and moves his arm in a motion like they're wiping a mirror off; the Driver is improperly steering the bus. I call this motion the "Karate Kid wax on wax off motion." Also if the Driver lets the steering wheel spin back after turning a corner, he's steering wrong.

Another common mistake that Drivers make is the placement of their thumbs. Their thumbs should not be on the inside of the steering wheel, but; on the outer rim of the steering wheel. This is because if the steering wheel spins back from the vehicle hitting debris in the road or a pothole the Driver will have control of the vehicle. This also will prevent the Driver from having their arms and hands entangled in the steering wheel if the steering wheel does spin back.

The correct way that a bus should be steered is what is called a "Push and Pull Method." It's ergonomically correct and helps prevent Driver injuries. In this method the Driver places his right hand on the steering wheel in or about the 3 "o" clock to the 5 "o" clock position. Their left hand is placed on the steering wheel in or about the 7 "o" clock to 9 "o" clock position. The Driver then pushes on the steering wheel or pulls on the steering wheel depending on which way that they want the vehicle to go. A series of short pushes and short pulls seem to work the best for me when maneuvering. This method takes a little getting used to, but: after a while you start to use the method naturally. The same method can be applied when driving a car.

Yea I know, that quite a few of the more experienced Drivers will say, "Hey, I'm safe and I haven't had an accident in years. How can I be steering wrong?" Granted your driving record may be good but what about your medical record. Chances are these Drivers complain about having a sore back; sore neck; carpal tunnel or other medical conditions that can be associated with poor driving techniques.

One last thing on driving that really has been bothering me: How can some Drivers sit in the Drivers seat all day; sitting on a piece of plastic or leather that's three to four inches thick? No really, that's what most guys do! If you haven't figured it out yet; I'm talking about their wallets. It's like sitting on a section of two by four on one side of your buttocks.

I know that when I drive I take my wallet out of my back pants pocket and keep it some where else. That somewhere else is someplace where my wallet is safe and convenient to get to. This safe place changes all the time. Some times I forget where it is. One day it's my lunch box the next day maybe my shirt pocket. Whatever!

In no specific order or reason I will try to convey to you twenty-seven short stories of incidents that occurred on a transit bus. I will not identify the ethnic origin of the individuals to which I'm speaking of, nor will I mention their names. This book is intended to be fun and informative. I am not by any means making fun of anybody, but; if the shoe fits, wear it! Enjoy!!!

TABLE OF CONTENTS

Chapter 1

EATING ON THE BUS

One of the many signs posted on the bus requests that the Passengers refrain from eating on the bus. Understanding this sign is not really that complicated and doesn't require much thought. Let me be a little bit sarcastic, like I usually am, and say I really enjoy it when Passengers sneak food on the bus and eat it while the bus is in motion. Oh yea, that's a mess waiting to happen. I especially look forward to cleaning up after people when they make messes. If a Passenger does accidentally drop a piece of food on the floor they don't bother to pick it up. What the Passenger does is kick the dropped food under the seat in front of them or under the seat that they're sitting in. These seats usually happen to be the back seats of the bus for obvious reasons.

The food that is safely tucked away under the seat now has a chance of becoming a permanent fixture on the bus. You see if the misplaced food doesn't get stepped on and gets tracked all over the bus; chances are that nobody will know that it's there. Many times the cleaning crew, while performing their busy duties, will over look little things like that. In time, the unforgotten food, after spawning and growing unknown molds and funguses, will finally get someone's attention.

This attention getter most often happens when a Passenger notices a strange odor on the bus. Sometimes the attention getter happens when a Passenger notices a mysterious object nestled on the bus floor in an obscure place.

The color and shape of these mysterious objects are usually determined by the changing seasons. Temperature extremes unquestionably have an affect on the mysterious objects. I came to the conclusion that if it is fall or winter then the undisclosed object is usually of dull or dark colors. Where as if it is summer or spring time the object in question appears to have brilliant and vibrant colors. This could be nature's way of camouflaging. The best I can tell is that there is no correlation between colors and odors. I've actually witnessed both types of specimens. In reality, I truly believe that both specimens can omit a fragrance that will bring tears to your eye and a lump in your throat.

There are objects that I have seen that fall into neither the color or odor category. These objects are just there. No one knows where they came from or how long they have been there. Heaven knows what they may mutate into. These objects are classified as "Just one of those unknown mysteries."

I realize that no one is perfect and we do what we have to do. Not going into any details, but; a while back one of my Passengers had a problem where he would eat food off the floor of the bus. The food that this Passenger ate from the floor included gum and candies. I had to tell him on numerous occasions not to. That really grossed me out. He did have some major issues so I won't go down that road.

A lady gets on my bus one morning and I notice that she has a bag of pastries from the local bakery in her left hand as she flashes me her monthly bus pass with her right hand. I noticed the logo on the pastry bag because I've been to that bakery many times before. Being experience with their foodstuffs I would say that everything that I have purchased from that bakery is exquisite. The bakery is known for products that are gooey, nutty, frosty and crumbly. There usually is an over abundances of whatever topping there is and the portions are huge. One cannot eat one of their products and not make a mess. Trust me on that!

The lady walked past me and sat down a couple seats behind me on the left side of the bus. People think that if they sit behind the Bus Driver; that the Bus Driver cannot see them. In reality, my interior mirror gives me a very good view of the entire interior of the bus. Even though the Driver has a good view of the bus coach, I would say that there are many blind spots on the bus. The seats directly behind the Driver fall into this category. Of course if someone wants to keep something out of the Drivers view, all they have to do is hold the item behind the backs of the seats or down low in front of them while they are seated on the bus. We Drivers can't see through the seats.

Anyways, after making sure everyone was seated and it was safe to continue my route; I closed the bus doors and safely merged into traffic. As I was driving I glanced into my interior mirror and watched as the lady, who had just boarded the bus, took a large pastry out of the bag that she was carrying and proceeded to take a big bite out of it that would make a crocodile proud! Not wanting to make a big deal out of it or cause a scene I said loudly, "Please don't eat on the bus."

Watching in the mirror, I saw the lady look up toward the Drivers area and at the same time put what was left of the pastry back into the bag. I thought that the incident was over. I watched in the mirror as the lady frantically chewed the food that was in her mouth. She was looking forward toward me and trying to talk and chew at the same time. While she was doing this she was making some really disgusting sounds. I really could not understand a word that she was trying to say. It took a minute or so before she could talk and I could understand her. I must say that she took a good bite out of that pastry. After she finished chewing and swallowing her food she said in a very loud sarcastic voice, "I'm not eating anything. Why are you picking on me?" She had one of those voices that used a lot of nasal punctuation. I thought of it as kind of annoying.

There were other Passengers on the bus and I did not want to argue with anyone about something so trivial. So again, not wanting to make a big deal out of it I said, "I'm not picking on anyone. All I'm asking is please don't eat on the bus. That's all!"

The lady yelled back, "I ain't eating nothing!!! Why are you looking at me and yelling at me?"

I said "Lady, I'm not yelling at anybody. All I'm asking is that you refrain from eating on the bus like everybody else. That's all!! This isn't worth getting upset and arguing over. OK?"

"No it's not OK! I ride the bus all the time and I never eat anything on the bus. You are just picking on me because you don't like me!"

Not wanting to continue arguing with her I needed to come up with a solution and I needed one fast. About that time the chime line sounded indicating one of the other Passengers wanted off at the next stop. Ah-ha, this was my way out. I pulled the bus over to the curb near the bus stop and opened the front and rear doors. I opened both doors because most of the Passengers were seated at the rear of the bus and it was more convenient for them to use the rear door rather than the front door.

A couple Passengers disembarked out of the rear door. As one of them was exiting the bus he waved to me and I waved back. This fellow was a regular rider and it was in his routine that when he got off the bus he would wave at the Bus Driver. After waving to the disembarking Passenger, I turned toward the lady whom I had been talking to about not eating on the bus. I spoke to her in a pleasant voice. I said to her "Before we continue this conversation, would you please come to the front of the bus. I want to show you something."

She looked at me as if I were trying to trick her. I said, "Please come to the front of the bus, I just want you to see something. I am not going to kick you off the bus or anything like that. I just want you to see something." After I said that to her it kind of toned things down. She reluctantly got up from her seat and walked to the front of the bus.

When she got up to the standee line, which is the line that extends across the aisle on the floor directly behind the Driver, I asked her to look in my rear view mirror. My rearview mirror is approximately three feet long and maybe nine inches wide. As I sat there in the Drivers seat watching; she leaned forward and look into the mirror. What she saw was the telltale sign of powdered sugar around her mouth. To top it off, her black sweater was also littered with sprinkles and crumbs from the aforementioned pastry.

I did not want to sit there and look like l was gloating, which I probably was. So I turned back in my seat toward the front of the bus. She looked at herself in the mirror for about three to five seconds and turned toward me. I was not expecting an apology or explanation, but; if she wanted to give me one I was more than willing to graciously accept it. No, that wasn't going to happen. What the lady did was snap her head toward me and look me directly in the face. Then without missing a beat she said, "I don't know what you're trying to show me, but; that stuff has been there since breakfast!"

I didn't say another word. I could tell that if anyone one was going to do any apologizing that it would have to be me and not her. And it sure wasn't going to be me! She returned to her seat content that she had won the argument and I humbly continued driving my bus route. I have made up my mind that the next time someone gets on my bus with a bag of pastries; I'm going to point out the no eating sign before they get past the standee line.

Chapter 2

LADY READING THE PAPER UPSIDE DOWN

There is such a variety of people that ride the bus that it would be extremely difficult to try to categorize every one of them. People want to be accepted as individuals regardless of what their income or social status is. It is just human nature. Many times when individuals do things out of their character, the end result is quite often unforgettable.

Morning time around the downtown bus station is usually pretty much the same year round. The Passengers that are at the bus station very early in the morning, first buses out, are typically regular Passengers who rely on the bus to get them to their jobs. In saying that, there is a combination of blue collar workers and white collar workers at the bus station at the same time. Most of the time the two groups intermingle harmoniously, but; occasionally there are heated discussions. If a problem does arise, the cause is usually one of the adult Passengers acting like a child rather than like the adult that their supposed to be. There is always one in every crowd.

By the time these two groups, the blue and white collar workers, have vacated the Transfer Center and are at their assigned jobs; the next wave of Passengers arrive at the Transit Station. The next wave of Passengers are the students. The student group includes: elementary students; middle school students; high school students and college age students. By the time that the students get to the downtown Transit Center the experienced adult bus riders are long gone. These adults don't want any part of this many Kids. These adults have experienced the Kids at their best; or should I say the Kids at their worst. The rowdiness, the profane language and smoking is just too much for a normal adult to put up with, especially if the adults are not use to being around Kids. All the Bus Drivers deal with the Kids in their own way. My way is to just ignore the Kids because I know that they will be gone in an hour or so. I do maintain order on my bus and the Kids know what I will and will not tolerate. They know that I'm not going to be intimidated and have no problem with reporting them and having their bus privileges taken away. They also know that I will respect them if they show me respect.

One morning on the first bus of the day I was waiting for our departure time to arrive. I sat in the Drivers seat enjoying my morning coffee and reading the sports page. The Passengers that were seated on the bus were doing their morning rituals. Some of the Passengers were reading whatever; some were listening to their radio or Ipod through their earphones while others just sat there thinking.

There were approximately ten Passengers on the bus at the time. It occurred to me that those that were reading were all reading the local paper. I knew this to be true because I had one of the newspapers too. As I glanced back through the coach section of the bus at the Passengers, I noticed something peculiar. The newspaper that they all were reading had a picture of a tall ship on the front page. This was an article about a Tall Ship Festival that our community was celebrating. This picture, of the tall ships, was in the upper left hand section of all the newspapers as the readers held the paper out in front of them as they read the newspaper. I noticed that one of the newspapers that one Passenger was reading, that the picture of the tall ship was upside down and in the lower right hand section of the newspaper.

I watched in amazement as the reader held the paper out in front of her and in sort of unisons turned the page of her paper when one of the other Passengers would turn the page of the paper that they were reading. I also noticed that the person who was reading the paper upside down was trying to emulate the Passenger seated across the aisle from her. The Passenger seated across the aisle from her was a regular Passenger and would always fold the newspaper in a special way that he could read the paper, but; in small sections at a time. I know this to be true because I have witnessed this Passenger fold his newspaper that way many times in the past.

Again, I am not judging people. All I'm doing is observing my Passengers actions. Anyways, the person that was reading the newspaper upside down is one of our special Passengers. She is not as fortunate as most people, but; her short comings are more than made up by her outgoing love for her fellow man. She has a wonderful attitude about everything. She is very inquisitive and at times she can be somewhat annoying to those that do not know her. She will strike up a conversation with anybody. Most of the time when she does strike up a conversation with someone, the conversation usually starts with her complimenting who ever she is talking to. All the Passengers that is familiar with her, kind of watch out for her well-being.

Let me continue, the time pasted quickly and before I knew it, it was time to depart. I announced over the internal loudspeaker that we were leaving the Transfer Center. I do this because then the Passengers won't be startled as the bus pulls out and there is less chance of anyone getting injured. Just a courtesy on my part I guess. Some people really do get engrossed in what their reading and lose tract of time: I know I do.

As we drove on with my assigned route, some of the Passengers kept reading the newspaper. I noticed that my special Passenger had put the newspaper away in one of her many tote bags that she carries and was just sitting there looking out the windows enjoying the scenery. I continued with my route. After driving about ten blocks or so I knew that the chime line would soon be sounded by my special Passenger. Knowing my Passenger routines has become a sort of hobby for me. Sure enough, the chime line sounded and my special Passenger wanted to be dropped off at the next bus-stop. This bus-stop incidentally was across the street from a large floral shop. My special Passenger, regardless of the weather, stopped here once a week to look at the pretty flowers and floral decorations. The next couple days after she stops at the florist, she always tells the Bus Drivers what the Driver misses by not stopping at the florist. This happens once a week to whoever is driving the bus route that she happens to be on. This is routine for her.

Well anyways, it usually takes her about a minute or so to gather all her belongings. She usually goes overboard on whatever she carries. Whatever the weatherman say's the weather will be; she will always be prepared for the worst. If the weatherman predicts a forecast of a chance for rain; to her it means that she must have in her possession a raincoat, a pair of boots and a large umbrella with her that day. Most of the time she forgets to empty her tote bags out and carry items for days. After gathering all her items she always come up to the Bus Driver and tells them thank you for the ride and for the Bus Driver to have a safe day.

I waited patiently for my special Passenger to come up to the front door. After she graciously thanked me and was working her way down the stairwell, with all her belongings in tow, to get off the bus, I stopped her to ask her a question. I did not want to or try to be condescending to her so I chose my words carefully. I then proceeded to ask her if she had seen anything interesting in the newspaper this morning. I was curious to hear her reply

She looked at me and thought for a moment. After gathering her thoughts she said, "I didn't see anything interesting, but; I did notice that all the pictures in the newspaper were upside down."

What could I say? I just sat there thinking about what she had said. Not wanting to hurt her feelings or discourage her, I didn't say another word. I didn't have the heart to tell her that she had the paper folder wrong.

Chapter 3

SHORT RIDE ON THE BIG BUS

I have not figured out yet if I think too much about things or if I think about things that I shouldn't think about. Sometimes I wonder if I'm the only one who actually notices things when things happen. Confused? I am.

I don't know if people are getting more lazy or if they have been lazy all the time and I never noticed it. I think that money has a lot to do with it. People who have money don't really understand what it is like not to have money if they have had money their entire life. It is people like this that do not really appreciate what they have and how fortunate they really are. I grew up in a family where we didn't have a lot of money, so; we never argued about something that we didn't have. We survived and got by the best that we could.

I pulled up to a busy bus stop one morning and there was a crowd of soon to be Passengers waiting patiently for the bus to arrive. I would say that there were ten or twelve people waiting for the bus. The weather outside was beautiful and it was just one of those gorgeous days where you would rather be outside than inside driving a bus. You know the kind of day I'm talking about. Just one of those days where you want to be any place but work.

One by one the people boarded the bus and either flashed their bus passes at me or dropped their fare into the fare-box. Most of the newly boarded Passengers either bid me good morning verbally or made some form of gesture acknowledging me. I responded to each of them with either a nod or a verbal "Good Morning."

The last person to board the bus at that stop was a woman whom I would guess to be in her late twenties or early thirties. She was casually dressed. She was wearing jeans, tennis shoes and a sweatshirt. All that she was carrying was a small purse, but; it was the small kind that women carry over their shoulders so it wasn't a burden for her to carry. There was nothing out of the ordinary that I observed about her.

As she boarded the bus she looked at her purse; said something to herself and then stood there for a second as if she was thinking of what to do next. After thinking and pausing for a moment, she opened her purse and started going through her change purse to get her bus fare. I sat there waiting and watching as she proceeded to inspect each and every coin, mostly pennies, before she dropped them into the fare-box. At the rate that she was putting the coins into the fare-box I could tell that it was going to take her a while for her to deposit her entire fare. I also figured out that this was going to cause me to be running later on my route than I already was. I didn't want to be impolite or rude to her because she seemed extremely frustrated about the entire situation at hand.

I remember thinking to myself, Lady this is just a bus ride there is no thinking involved here. Put your money in the box and have a seat. No big deal.

I did not know what was going on. It was obvious to me that she wasn't use to riding the bus. I politely said to her, "Excuse me Mame, but; I have a schedule to keep. Would it be possible to please hurry up?"

The lady looked at me and said, "I'm sorry, I'm going as fast as I can. I have to look at all these coins because I'm a Numismatic and just realized that I grabbed my wrong coin purse. There could be a valuable coin in here and I don't want to put one into the fare-box and lose it."

I said, "OK, but please hurry." By the way, those of us that don't know what a Numismatic is, they are Coin Collectors. I sat there watching as the lady sorted out each and every coin that she handled. She handled each coin very carefully and watchfully. Most of the coins that she inspected would be put back into her purse while others were being dropped into the fare box. She looked up toward me as she was sorting her change and said, "I'm so sorry. It's OK to put pennies into the fare box, right?"

I looked at her and said" Yes Mame, it takes pennies. You do realize that the coins are tallied automatically by the fare-box?"

She replied, "I didn't know that. How much more do I owe?"

I looked at the LCD readout on the fare box because it gave the total of the amount of coins that she had deposited. I said, "You have put in thirty two cents so far. The adult fare is one dollar. Could you please hurry up a little bit because this is really causing me to run behind schedule?" Heck I don't need someone to help me run behind schedule because I am good at doing it myself.

After about a minute or so, it seemed like forever to me, she finally dropped the last of her fare into the fare-box. She kept tract of what she was depositing by constantly looking at the LCD calculated total of the coins on the fare-box window. By now, she had been standing there approximately four to five minutes. I know that I probably made her nervous by constantly looking at my watch, but; I needed her to hurry up. A few of the Passengers were asking me if I could call and have the other buses hold at the Transfer Center because they needed to make the transfer. I told them that the other buses would wait until I got there. I'm sure all these little comments out loud were bothering the Numismatic Lady, but she completed her task and went and sat down next to the other Passengers.

After she was seated, I safely merged the bus into traffic and continued with my route. The bus stops are placed about every two blocks or so along my route. The distances between the bus stops vary depending on traffic patterns. In this case the next bus stop was about one city block from where I had just stopped. The chime line immediately sounded indicating that someone wanted off at the next stop. I put my flashers on; pulled the bus to the curb and opened the doors. Much to my surprise the Numismatic Lady, the lady who had just taken five minutes of my time by checking each of her coins, was wanting off at this stop. I could not believe what was happening. She had spent more time going though those coins than she did riding on the bus. She could have walked here faster. After the bus was completely stopped, the Numismatic Lady came to the front of the bus and graciously thanked me for the ride. I was confused. It usually doesn't take much to confuse me, but; this was ridiculous.

I thought to myself for a moment as she stood there. I immediately thought that one of the other Passengers had made an unprofessional comment to her and that she was upset. But that didn't seem to be the case. I know for a fact that some Passengers can be real obnoxious and rude with their comments. I don't go for that on my bus. I asked her, "Did another Passenger make a comment to you and is that why you are getting off the bus?"

She looked at me with a funny look on her face and said, "Heavens no! Everybody was nice to me. This is the bus stop that I had planned to get off at."

I said," You're the lady that just got on the bus at the last stop, right."

She said to me," Yes. Did I do something wrong?"

Not wanting to make her feel bad or more importantly not wanting myself to look like a fool I said," No, No, No you're fine; it is probably just me. I think that I am experiencing a senior moment or something. Please accept my sincere apology. Have a nice day."

She said, "Thank you and you also have a nice day. I really enjoyed my bus ride with you."

I watched in disbelief as she disembarked the bus and was walking away from the bus stop. As she was walking away, she turned and waved bye to me. I waved back. When it was safe, I merged the bus back into traffic. Some of the more observant Passengers asked why she had gotten off the bus. I said that she told me that that was her stop. Most of the other Passengers shook their head, rolled their eyes or had a dumbfounded look on their faces.

I guess that one block was just too far for that lady to walk. I think that brings us back to what I was saying at the beginning of this story. People who have money sometimes don't use common sense because it is easier to pay someone to do something for you rather than to do it yourself. In this case that meant paying one dollar for a really short ride on a really big bus.

Chapter 4

THE RUMMAGE SALE

I get the opportunity to meet a lot of people when I'm driving the bus. I think that the most interesting folks that I have met are the elderly. This group seems to come up with the most interesting stories that I've ever heard. They talk about everything from the good old days to the present. I especially enjoy the stories of the past. You can see the elderly reliving their youth in their eyes. Their eyes twinkle when reminiscing. Many times after they tell me stories of the past they will just sit there and not say another word for a few minutes. I think that they are actually reliving a time in their life through daydreams. Good for them. Many a time after they have told me stories they seem to be in a happier mood and occasionally wipe tears from their eyes.

I had the privilege to meet a lady who was ninety-eight years young. She use to ride the bus daily. If I hadn't known her exact age, I would have guessed her to be in her late sixties or early seventies. She was really in good shape and her mind was sharp. Of course she didn't move really fast, but; she did get along at a good pace. She told me a lot of things about herself. She told me that when her husband of fifty years passed away, that she made a promise to herself and him. She vowed never remarry, but; would date other men. After all she said a woman has needs. I told her please don't go into detail, that's too much information for me to handle. She told me stuff like that all the time. She said that I reminded her of her youngest brother. He by the way is in his late eighties.

One day she got on my bus and just the way she was acting I knew that there was something bothering her. Not wanting to appear nosy I said to her, "So how are things going this fine day?"

She looked at me and said very seriously, "Marty, can I ask you for some advice?" I was flabbergasted; I had no idea of how to give advice to a ninety eight year old person. I wasn't really sure of what she wanted to ask me. I figured what the heck, if she wants your advice, just be honest and do the best you can. So I said to her, "How can I help you?"

She started telling me about her job at the hospital. She was a Greeter and would answer questions and help visitors find patients rooms. The majority of the time she spent at her job; she was sitting at a desk and talking to people who needed directions. She told me how much she like working there and how much she appreciated getting out of the house and working for a living. By the way, she was a volunteer greeter and she didn't get paid anything for her work. Her job had her working two hours a week, year round for the past twenty two years. She said that she didn't want to disappoint anyone and was trying to figure out how to tell her boss that she wanted to quit. She asked me, "Marty, what should I do? How do I tell my boss that I don't want to work there anymore?"

I thought to myself, hey that's a no brainier. When you get home call your boss and tell them that your ninety-eight years old and want to start taking it easy. That would have been my answer, but; I knew that wasn't the answer that she wanted me to tell her. I knew that there was more to this than she was telling me.

I said to her, "OK what's really bothering you?"

She looked at me and said, "I really can get along with anyone, but; there is this one woman who works at the hospital with me that I do not wish or want to be around. She works the same hours and day that I work and I do not want to associate with her. A while back someone stole all my clothes out of the washing machine and dryer at the apartment complex where I live. I wash my clothes twice a month and wear fresh clothes every day. After all my clothes were taken, I had to go out and spend hundreds of dollars on a new wardrobe. I was really irritated that anyone would want to steal an old ladies clothing. Do you know that they even took my under garments? By the way do you know what ladies undergarments cost?"

I sheepishly said, "No."

She continued telling me all about how mad she was, but; she proclaimed that she was a God faring woman and forgave the dirty, lowdown, no-good thief that took all her clothes. She said, "If they need those clothes more than me; they can have them!"

I knew that she was mad by the tone of her voice. I figured that she needed someone to vent to so I was just going to be there for her. I was curious about where this story was going and I asked her, "So, why do you want to quit your job?"

She looked at me and said, "Will you please let me finish telling the story!"

"Please continue", I humbly exclaimed. I didn't think that I had interrupted her; but she must have thought that I did. Well anyways she started talking again. She said," I didn't think that anyone that I knew would stoop so low and take anything that I had, but; another lady that lives in our apartment complex did. All she would have had to do is ask me and I would have willingly given her anything that I had. But she chose to steal it and then deny it. Not only did she steal my stuff, but; she stole items from the other people that live in our apartment complex."

I said, "How do you know that it was her that took the stuff?"

My elderly friend gave me a very stern look and exclaimed, "Our apartment complex had a community rummage sale and my so called close friend was selling all the clothes that she had stolen from all the other tenants. One of the other tenants and I went to the rummage sale and lo and behold she was selling all of our belongings. I had monogrammed clothing that she was selling as hers. I went up to her at the rummage sale and asked her where she had gotten all these clothes from. She told me that she had these clothes all her life and that she felt that it was time to get rid of them. I couldn't believe that my friend would treat me like that and lie to me. Maybe she has some issues that I am not aware of."

The elderly woman sat there and looked at me as if I knew what to do. To be honest with you, I didn't know what to say. Finally after a few seconds I said to the elderly woman, "Well live and learn, I guess. You know, that it probably won't be worth the effort trying to get your clothes back. All that's going to happen is that you will get upset, right?" The elderly woman shook her head in agreement. I continued," You probably should try to avoid that lady and try not to get upset over the situation as it is. As for your quitting your job, I think that is the wrong thing for you to do. If you talk to your boss and tell them that you want a different day that they will probably help you out. I wouldn't even mention your concerns about the other lady. Just keep positive and be the lovely lady that you are. I'm sure things will work out." After saying my piece; my friend just sat there looking out the bus window. I could tell that she was thinking, so; I knew that it was time for me to shut my mouth and just drive the bus.

We got to the elderly woman's bus stop and she pulled the chime line. Before she got off the bus, she turned to me and said, "Thank you Marty for your advice. That's exactly what I was going to do, but; I just needed someone to reassure me."

Quite awhile has pasted since she and I had that conversation on the bus. I saw my elderly lady friend a while ago. Because I changed jobs, I don't see a lot of my friends as often as I wish I could. I think that she was as pleased to see me as I was to see her. During our brief conversation, my elderly friend filled me in on how her life has been the last few years. She told me: She still works at the hospital once a week; she still lives in the same senior apartment complex and she recently celebrated her one hundredth birthday and is looking forward to one hundred and one. Life is good!!!

Chapter 5

Boys will be Boys

It is said that curiosity killed the cat. I don't really know a lot about that, but: I do know that being curious has gotten me in hot water throughout my entire life. It is human nature to explore and try to understand things that you don't know. I think that young boys are probably the best example of why that cat gets killed everyday. In our early development years, that perhaps is the only time in our lives, which gives us the opportunity to truly plead ignorance to a lot of things. When Kids ask questions it's because they don't know. We adults take things for granted, but; when you're a kid everything is new. That's were curiosity comes into play.

I can recall a while back when four young boys, maybe ten or eleven years of age, boarded my bus. I remember that it was a Saturday because the boys could not use their school issued bus passes and had to pay a regular student fare. It is one of those thought out bureaucratic policies where if it's not a school day, then the Kids have to pay student fare because the bus pass is for getting them to and from school only. So if the Kids want to go to the library or museum on Saturdays or school days off they got to pay. I figure that they could be doing a lot worse things than riding the bus, but; whatever.

So the boys get on the bus, paid their fare and politely ask me if I could drop them off as close to the museum as possible. They were all in a good mood and were playfully joking amongst themselves. You know how boys act when they're with their friends. I said to the boys as they walked past me to go to the rear of the bus, "You guys keep the noise down and no horseplay; OK?"

They all gave a resounding, "OK" to my request.

The boys walked to the rear of the bus and they all sat down on one side of the rear seat of the bus. The rear seat on this bus was u shaped. The group of boys sat across the aisle from another Passenger who was seated on the rear seat opposite from where they were seated. At that time there were at least five other Passengers on the bus. All of those Passengers were seated toward the front of the bus. Every thing seemed normal and nothing out of the ordinary.

As I drove the bus on route, something wasn't right. I didn't hear those boys that had boarded earlier. Usually the Bus Driver has to ask groups of Kids to at least keep it down once, but; not today. I glanced into the mirror and saw all four boys just sitting on the back seat. They were not talking amongst themselves; all they were doing was just sitting there. I figured hey, these are some well behaved Kids. Then I came to my senses and said to myself, "You had better keep an eye on these Kids, just to be sure."

As we continued the route I kept a watchful eye. They all just sat there not doing anything. Heck, they weren't even talking to each other. We finally got near the museum that they were going to and I said out loud, "Hey guys we're at your destination." I watched in the interior mirror as they spoke between themselves. When I stopped the bus at the bus stop, one of the boys walked to the front of the bus. By this time the boys and the other Passenger that was seated on the rear seat of the bus were the only Passengers on board.

The boy that walked to the front of the bus said to me, "We decided to go someplace else. If we owe you more money just let us know."

I said, "Ok."

The young man walked back toward the rear of the bus to where he had been seated and sat down. He and his friend spoke between themselves and sat there as if they were mesmerized by something. I thought that maybe they knew the Passenger that was seated back there with them and was on their best behavior. I said to myself, "those boys are up to something. I've got to find out what's up." There was a small strip mall about a block away and there was a bus stop there. I figure that I'd stop the bus and check things out for myself.

When I arrived at the strip mall; I pulled up to the bus stop, put my flashers on and opened the front and rear doors. I glanced into my interior mirror and noticed that there was no activity from the rear seat. There were just the boys and the other Passenger sitting back there. I got up from the Drivers seat and started to walk the coach of the bus as if I were just checking the bus out. We Drivers do this a few times a day to look and see if anybody left anything on board or made some kind of mess that we needed to know about.

As I got to the rear seat of the bus the boys watched me as I approached. It was then that I realized that the Passenger that was seated across the aisle from the boys was a woman who was sleeping on the bus. To put it nicely, the lady was perhaps in her forties and was no spring chicken. To top it off, the ladies blouse was unbuttoned and her cleavage and breasts was exposed. The boys were getting their own private peep show. There wasn't really that much to see and the ladies breasts wasn't fully exposed, but; to those young boys it was a fantasy come true. I looked at the boys and said" You guys should be ashamed of yourselves! Go sit up at the front of the bus." The boys got up and walked to the front of the bus. As each one of the boys passed the sleeping lady they gave one more look at her partially exposed breasts. I walked up to the sleeping woman and said rather loudly, "excuse me mame." She woke up immediately. I then said to her, "You cannot sleep on the bus and you need to fix your blouse because you're exposing yourself."

The lady sat up from her slouched position and looked at me. She then glanced down at her open blouse and without more ado started to button the unbutton buttons. As she was fastening her blouse she looked at me and said to me, "You Pervert!! Did you get a good look?"

I said to her, "Lady I just walked back here and saw you sleeping. All I did was wake you up because you were sleeping on the bus. If you want, I can make a big deal out of this and have the cops get involved. What do you want me to do?"

She sat there for a moment gathering her thoughts. She said, "Where are we at?"

I told here where we were and she said to me, "I'll get off here. This is close to where I wanted to go anyways. She got up from her seat and exited the bus. As she was getting off the bus I told her to be careful and to have a nice day. She just looked at me and shook her head. My only Passengers on the bus now were the four boys. I didn't say anything to them as I walked by them and got into the Drivers seat. The boys just sat there, they knew that I was disgusted with their actions.

I gathered my thoughts and said to the boys, "So you guys still going to the museum?"

I watched in the mirror as the boys talked between themselves. After much discussion, one of them spoke up and said, "Yes. We decide that we should go to the museum."

I said, "OK, but; you guys need to go to the end of the line with me and I'll drop you off on the way back. OK?" They all agreed to my request. I wanted to do it this way because then I knew that they would go to the museum and also they would not encounter the lady that was sleeping on the bus. I didn't want to take the chance of her giving the boys a hard time. You never know how people are going to react, so; why take chances.

I dropped the boys off at the museum on my return trip. As each one of the boys got off the bus, they thanked me for the bus ride. Each one of them had a huge smile on their face and the look of pure satisfaction. I'm sure that this is one bus ride that they will remember and talk about the rest of their lives. Not to mention the stories that they will be telling to their friends, after all; boys will be boys.

Chapter 6

THE BUTTERFLY LADY

I find it intriguing the way things work out. How many times in our life do we say something, in passing to strangers, and not realize how those words affect that person's life. I really get a chance to meet a variety of individuals while I'm performing my duties. Everybody has a story. I try to picture what their stories are, not prejudging mind you, before they tell me their story. A Bus Driver is like a Bartender when it comes to hearing people's life story. After all we are there, in the Bus Drivers case the Passengers and in the Bartenders case his patrons, captured audiences. The bartender gets the stories told to them when their patrons are vulnerable and at a slight disadvantage. This is mostly cause by too much consumption of alcohol by the bar patrons. In the Bus Drivers case; most of the Passengers just feel that it is an easy vent for them. A sympathetic ear if I may say. After all, the Bus Driver does start the conversations when they welcome Passengers on the bus. All it takes is a friendly salutation and it opens the flood gates of information. As always, too much information isn't always good.

Before our city Transit Department took on a fleet of new buses, we Drivers had to deal with equipment that was poorly maintained. It was not uncommon for the bus to just stop running and stall in the middle of the street. Many times the buses had Passengers on board when they stalled in traffic. The memo driven excuses that we Drivers got from the Maintenance Department on why the transit equipment broke down varied from: it's too hot outside; it's too cold outside; it's raining or it's snowing. The answer that we got from the honest Mechanic's was that the buses were a piece of junk and that the buses needed to be replaced. We very seldom got this response because nobody wanted to fess up to the situation even though they all knew it to be true. Nobody wanted to make waves and besides it was easier to try to blame the Bus Driver when things went wrong rather than to admit the truth.

Several of the Passengers that use the Transit System are confined to wheelchairs. Most of the time the wheelchair confined Passengers will give a courtesy call to the Transit Department saying that they are wheelchair bound and will be boarding a certain bus at a certain time and at a certain bus stop. This gives the Bus Driver advance notification that they will be getting a wheelchair. There are Federal rules that must be adhered to when transporting wheelchair confined Passengers. With the old buses that we had, certain buses were not equipped to handle wheelchairs properly. Many of the old buses had mechanical lifts to handle wheelchairs, but; most of the time those lifts either didn't work or stopped working when in use, just like the buses did. When the equipment failed to work properly, it usually put the Bus Driver and the wheelchair Passengers in an awkward position.

Now the entire city Transit Department's fleet is all wheelchair accessible. The fix on the new buses was to have ramps rather then lifts. Great Idea!!! These ramps worked out much better because they could be manually activated if the mechanical or electrical system failed to work properly.

One day a while back, I received a call from Dispatch notifying me that I would be getting a wheelchair at a senior living center that was on my route. This incidentally happened in the time frame just prior to the Transit Department acquiring new buses. I knew the condition of my wheelchair lift and informed Dispatch that the last time that I tried to use the lift that it didn't work properly. My Dispatcher told to me to pull over at the next bus stop and activate the lift to make sure that it worked properly. Dispatch called doing that a "test run." We Drivers called it a waste of time and energy because it really didn't mean anything. I pulled the bus over at the next bus stop to do a practice lift and the wheelchair lift worked flawlessly. That was no surprise. I informed my Dispatcher that everything seemed Ok at the time and that I was on my way to the senior complex to try to pick the wheelchair Passenger up. Being proactive my Dispatcher told me everything will work fine. Think positive! I remember saying to myself, "Easy for you to say Pal, you don't have to deal with the Passengers."

When I arrived at the senior complex, there was a small group of seniors waiting for the bus. Among them was a lady confined to a wheelchair. Little did I know that this lady and I would become good friends in such a short time. I pulled the bus up to the bus stop and announced to the Passengers that were on board that we would be under way shortly after I picked up this group of seniors. They all knew the routine that I had to go through because of the wheelchair Passenger. I put my flashers on and opened both the front and rear doors of the bus. The group of those not confined to a wheelchair came on board the bus through the front door, while; the lady in the wheelchair went to the rear door of the bus through the direction of the group of seniors who knew where the wheelchair chair lift was. After I checked the group's bus passes and they were all seated, I went to activate the wheelchair lift at the rear door of the bus.

The lady in the wheelchair was very friendly and talkative as I secured the wheelchair to the lift. I kept to task securing the wheelchair while she sat there telling me how she was new to the area and this was her first bus ride in our city. She told me that she had moved here from Mississippi to be close to her only child. I listened and worked while she spoke. She said she really liked the snow and was looking forward to the change in seasons. While I was securing the wheelchair to the lift; I tried to explain to the woman what the process was to get her and her wheelchair onto the bus. She listened intently and told me that she understood what I had told her. It was snowing heavy now and the snowflakes were the large fluffy ones. My main concern was to get her on the bus and out of the elements.

After making sure that she and her wheelchair were secure; I activated the wheelchair lift. The wheelchair lift worked smoothly until I got the lady and the wheelchair about three feet off the ground. Then without any warning the wheelchair lift stopped working. The lady in the wheelchair gave me a concerned look and I reassured her that everything was going to be fine. I knew exactly what was happening because this had happened before. I was just hoping that the lift would start working right away.

I tried unsuccessfully to get the lift working and determined that I needed help from Dispatch. The lady in the wheelchair just sat there watching me work. She was calm and seemed to have complete faith in me. I kept reassuring her that things would be ok. I contacted Dispatch and told them of my predicament. They told me to hold tight and that they would contact the maintenance garage for assistance.

It was really snowing heavy by now. The only good thing about the snow was that it was the light fluffy stuff rather than the heavy wet stuff. The other Passengers on the bus just sat there watching me as I tried to cope with the situation that I was in.

I spoke to the lady in the wheelchair and made sure that she was comfortable and warm. I asked her if there was anything that I could do to make her more comfortable. She said that she had a blanket in her wheelchair pouch and asked me to place the blanket over her head to keep her warm and dry because of the snow. I took the blanket out of the wheelchair pouch and I placed it over her head and also wrapped the blanket around her wheelchair to keep her warm and dry. After I placing the blanket over her, the only thing that was exposed to the elements was her face. Jokingly, I told her that she looked like a butterfly coming out of a cocoon. We both laughed at my silly comment. Little did I know that this comment would come back to haunt me. Some of the other Passengers moved to the rear of the bus to talk to her and keep her company while I was on the radio at the front of the bus speaking to my Dispatcher and keeping them abreast of the situation.

Dispatch called me back and informed me that a mechanic was on the way. I was told to handle the situation as best as I could until help arrived. They knew that I couldn't go anyplace, let alone close the doors on the bus because of a mechanical interlock that activated when the lift is in use. There the bus sat with the front and rear doors open exposing everyone on board to the snowy elements. The wheelchair bound Passenger was hanging out of the back door by four feet positioned on a mechanical lift that wouldn't budge.

I went to the lift and knelt down by the lady who was in the wheelchair. I didn't want to stand over her cowering, so; I knelt by her side and looked at her face to face when I spoke to her. I kept apologizing to her about the situation. She started to laugh and told me not to worry about it because she was a tough old bird and she could take a lot of abuse. I laughed at her comment, but; I could hear the apprehension in her voice. I knelt by her for about twenty minutes before the replacement bus showed up. During that time, I tried my best to keep the snow off of her and keep her mind occupied. Keeping her occupied was the easy part. Keeping the snow off of her was a waste of time because it was snowing so heavy.

The lady in the wheelchair and I spoke about everything that you can imagine while we waited. The topics included: Cabbage patch dolls, southern cooking and life in general. That day, I learned more about grits; green fried tomatoes and southern cooking then I ever thought that I would need to know. I thought it to be rather interesting and I'm always the one for useless information.

The replacement bus arrived and the mechanic and I swapped buses. The mechanic was going to take charge of the disabled bus and get the lift working. He was also going to take all the Passengers that were on board the disabled bus to the locations that they were trying to get to. He was doing this because of the inconvenience that they faced due to the malfunctioning chairlift. I on the other hand would have to continue my transit route. Incases like this, we Drivers drive the bus to where the bus schedule says that the bus is supposed to be at that time.

I told the Passengers before I got off the bus that I was truly sorry for their inconvenience. The mechanic was working feverishly on the lift as I drove away. He told me later that it took him about ten minutes to get the wheelchair lift working. As I drove away: the lady who was on the lift in the wheelchair smiled and waved to me. She still had the blanket over her head and it was now covered with snow.

Every time, after that day, whenever I saw that wheelchair bound woman we would talk like we knew each other forever. Whenever she was on my bus, as a matter of fact this applied to anybody that is in a wheelchair, I had to follow federal guidelines about securing wheelchairs during transit. Each and every time that I removed the last of the restraints that secured her wheelchair in transit; I would lean over and whisper in her ear and say, "Your free little butterfly, fly away." It was a playful little game that we both enjoyed. She was the only one of my Passengers that I did this for and she knew it. I would do this each and every time that she got off my bus. If I would forget to say it, she would not move her wheelchair until I said that little phrase. After I would say the phrase she would smile, laugh and giggle like a little school girl and ride away in her wheelchair. We shared many playful moments like this together. I know we both really enjoyed them.

My friend in the wheelchair was very sick. After a very courageous battle with her disease, it eventually got out of control and she finally succumbed to her illness. I was very sad for losing her. I don't go to the funerals of all those who rode on my bus, but; this one was very different. She had gone from the category of bus Passenger into the realm of being my friend. She was a very special person to me even though I had known her for such a short period of time. I spoke to my wife about my concerns of going to my lady Passenger's funeral and my wife, my best friend, told me to do what I thought was best for me. I decided to go to my wheelchair friend's funeral wake.

The next evening after work, with my head held high and a heavy heart; I walked into the local funeral home. After entering the funeral home I was greeted by a young man who directed me to the room where my friend's service was being held. As I walked into the room I noticed that there was no casket. I assumed that she had been cremated. There were about twenty or so people gathered around a table near the front of the room. I figured that this was where her remains were. Not wanting to impose on the group; I sat down in a chair at the rear of the room and waited for the right time to go up to the table that they were all standing around. I knew that the right time for me would be when nobody else was up there by the table.

As I sat there waiting, I looked around the funeral parlor room at the numerous floral bouquets that were placed around the room. I got a lump in my throat and a tear in my eye as I noticed a theme. The theme was butterflies. There were literally hundreds of butterflies being used to decorate the room. There were butterflies made of silk, ceramic, wood and paper. Many of the floral arrangements were shaped like butterflies. Their brilliant colors gave the room an uplifting feeling and I sensed a feeling of peace surrounding me. Never before in my life had I ever felt such a surreal sense of peace. I couldn't hold back the tears and cried as

I thought about my friend and our shared memories. I know that Guys aren't supposed to cry, but; I did and have no regrets about it.

I composed myself and after a few minutes the people that were by the front table moved to a different location and were socializing. With tears in my eyes and my heart broken, I respectfully walked up to the table to pay my last respects to my dear friend. As I walked up to the table in the front of the room I saw a cremation urn and an old framed picture on the table. The photograph that was on the table was of a young woman dancing. It was my friend. I never thought of her in that light because I only knew her in her wheelchair. I thought that I really knew her, but; obviously I was wrong. She never told me that she was a dancer. She was without a doubt a very attractive young lady whom loved to dance and that picture said it all. I was mesmerized by the picture.

As I stood there looking at the picture, a young man came up to me and introduced himself as my friend's son. I started to give my condolences to the man and got to the point in my testimonial where I said that my name was Marty and that I was his mother's friend, the Bus Driver. That was when the man interrupted me and said, "Did you know that my mom thought of you as her best friend?"

I reached out my hand in friendship and said, "What? I don't understand." He smiled at me as he shook my hand. He then told me that his mother had told him about that infamous snowy day on the bus and the little phrase about the butterfly that we always shared together. He proceeded to tell me that his mother said that I was one of the nicest people that she had ever met and that she really thought of me as one of her best friends. She said that she never met anyone in her life that was so friendly.

He laughed as he tried to hold back his tears. He said that his mother started collecting butterflies shortly after that infamous snowy day. He said that Mom thought of herself as a butterfly coming out of a cocoon since the day. He said that she told him that it gave her hope. He thanked me for being his mother's friend. I didn't know what to say. I again gave him my condolences and said that I needed to be excused. When I left the room I had many tears in my eyes and a lump in my throat that actually hurt.

If I hadn't gone to my friends wake, I would never have known the entire story. That night as I drove home I thought of how my joking comments had made a difference in somebody's life. It made me happy, but; a little bit sad too. I kept thinking to myself: What would I have done if I had known sooner how she truly felt?

It has been a while now since that night and I think of my departed friend quite often. Every time I'm working and I disconnect the restraints from a wheelchair on my bus, I think of saying that little phrase that I had shared with my friend, but; I don't. I don't think that my friend, the Butterfly Lady, would mind if I used the phrase on someone else, but; I think of it as something special just between her and I, so I don't. It is times like that when I really miss her. May she rest in peace.

Chapter 7

Hey, where's my shopping cart?

I wish that I had a quarter for every time that I tried to help someone, only; to have them act rude to me because of their ignorance. I know that it has happened to everyone at one time or another. People want other people to mind their own business. I agree with them to a point, but; when their business interferes with my business then their business is my business. Make sense?

I was parked at the end of the line one day at a very busy shopping center. I was waiting for departure time to arrive, so; after checking the bus coach I was just sitting in the Drivers seat of the bus enjoying the day. It was rather windy outside, but; overall a very pleasant day. I watched as the busy Shoppers left the safety of the shopping center indoors and exited in to the traffic congested parking lot.

When Shoppers are walking in the parking lot they feel that they are invincible. I've watched Pedestrians crossing at the crosswalk at shopping centers walk right in front of moving cars. Yea, I know that Pedestrians have the right of way, but; getting hit by a car doesn't necessary have to happen to prove their point. I would say that they don't care about their personal safety. When the Shoppers are exiting the stores, all they care about is getting back to their vehicles and unloading their fully loaded shopping carts into said vehicle. While walking through the parking lot they are focused on one thing. That one thing is remembering where they parked.

Once the Shoppers find their vehicle they switch to another mode. That mode is empting all the newly purchased items into their vehicle. After the Shoppers are done loading up their vehicles they need to discard the shopping cart. Sounds easy right? The shopping centers have conveniently constructed shopping cart corrals stations throughout the parking lot, but; why use them when it's easier to just abandon the cart anyplace in the parking lot?

As I'm sitting on the bus watching all the busy people, I was particularly interested with one shopper. What caught my eye was that she was using two shopping carts at one time. She had one loaded shopping cart that she was pushing in front of her with her right hand and she was pulling another fully loaded shopping cart with her left hand. She was obviously in a hurry and was trying to do everything in what I figure out to be one trip.

I watched as the lady made her way though the parking lot toward her vehicle: which incidental turned out to be a minivan.

Once at the minivan she put the shopping cart that she was pushing at the rear door of the minivan. She then situated the cart so that it was against the minivan and hanging out into the parking lot aisle. After she felt that the shopping cart wasn't going anyplace she took the shopping cart that she was pulling to the side door of the minivan. The side doors and rear door of the minivan were activated by a box on her key ring. I assumed this to be true because the doors all opened at the same time.

The lady was now standing on side of her minivan with the shopping cart that she was pulling between her and the shopping cart that she had placed by the rear door of the minivan. I had a good view of the entire situation from where I was parked with the bus. The lady didn't realize that when she opened the doors of the minivan that the shopping cart that was at the back door was now pushed away from the minivan The parking lot was slanted to allow for proper water drainage and that is when basic physic's took over. The wheeled shopping cart started to roll away from the minivan. The shopping cart was headed away from the minivan and toward parts unknown. The lady didn't have a clue that her second shopping cart was rolling away. The minivan was blocking her view of the runaway shopping cart.

I could see the whole story playing out not more than fifty feet away from me. I said to myself, "Do something!" What was I going to do? I was seated in a bus and there was not much that I could do. I sat there thinking. I came to the conclusion that if I honked the horn on the bus that I could warn the lady that her shopping cart was rolling away from her. So I honked the bus horn for about five seconds until the lady by the minivan looked my way. While she was looking at me, I pointed toward her runaway cart. She looked at me for a second and then went back to loading her items into the minivan. She obviously didn't care what I was pointing at.

By now the runaway shopping cart had picked up some speed. I watched as it sped through that parking lot; glanced off of a light pole and then briefly came to an abrupt stop. Some of the items that were in the cart were now lying in the parking lot because of the collision with the light pole. The cart was now facing backwards and started to roll again. The front wheels of the cart was on swivels and the cart was now traveling backward with the front of the cart swaying back and forth as the cart picked up speed through the parking lot for a second time. I again honked the bus horn to get the woman's attention. I know that it was rather rude of me honking the bus horn, but; what other option did I have? I thought of my encounter with a red sports car awhile back and how that Driver didn't quite like the sound of bus horn either. Ah, I'm over that one.

The lady, whose cart was rolling away, looked at me. With all good intentions I motioned to her through the open Drivers window of the bus. I was making a pointing motion to make her aware of the situation. I didn't yell out anything. What did she do? She yelled an obscenity at me gave me the middle finger. I sat there in the bus seat laughing. I tried to help her, but: now she was on her own. I glanced at my watch and still had a few minutes before I had to continue with my route. That was good because I wanted to see how this situation was going to end.

I glanced at the runaway shopping cart as it made its way to the far end of the parking lot. The shopping cart was flying through the parking lot at a pretty good speed by now. There must have been a curb at the end of the lot because when the runaway cart hit it, the shopping cart instantly turned over on its side empting most of its contents. By now the lady had finished unloading the first shopping cart and was abandoning that cart in front of the minivan. There was a cart corral not ten feet away and it must have been too far for her to take the empty cart. Whatever!

I watched as she walked to the rear of the minivan expecting to find her other shopping cart. When she got to the back of the minivan by the rear door, the shopping cart was gone. She panicked. She stood there at the rear of the minivan looking around for her missing shopping cart. She even looked under the minivan. She was really frantic and panicking. I said to myself, "You gotta do something." What did I do? I did the only thing that I could do, I honked the bus horn.

The lady looked at me and must have figured out that I was trying to help her. She left her minivan and came running up to the open window by where I was seated. She started yelling at me and said, "What did you do with my groceries?"

I sat there in the bus not really believing what she was saying. I said to her, "Oh, you mean that shopping cart that I tried to warn you about that was rolling away from your minivan."

She looked at me as if she was confused and said, "What?"

I said to her, "You know what shopping cart I'm talking about. It is the one that was rolling away from your minivan that I tried to warn you about. Remember you gave me the finger instead of looking the way I was pointing."

She said to me, "Oh no; you were just trying to help me. I'm so sorry. I thought that you were making fun of me or something. Where is my shopping cart at?"

I pointed to the end of the parking lot. She immediately turned and looked that way and saw her shopping cart lying on its side. I asked her if she wanted me to help her because I had a few minutes before I had to leave and do my route. I really didn't have the time, but; I kind of felt bad for her. She said," Yes please!" I told her that I would drive the bus over by her upturned cart and she should get her minivan and meet me over there. I then told her about the items by the light pole. She said that she would get those items first and then meet me by the shopping cart. "Sounds like a plan to me," I said.

I drove my bus over to the overturned shopping cart and waited for the minivan to show. After she drove next to the overturned cart; I got out of the bus and helped here load up her minivan. After helping her, she offered me some money. I declined her offer. I told her that it was part of my job duties to help people. As I drove away to continue with my route she pulled up along side the bus with her minivan. She waved to me and honked her horn at me. I really didn't get upset with someone honking their horn at me like I've seen other people get when I honked my horn at them. I wonder why?

Chapter 8

Hey, gotta a smoke?

Kids sure act different when they're with their friends than they do if they're with their parents. I get the opportunity to see how these young adults act in both situations. The only question is; can the young adults keep both of their audiences satisfied while they're trying to make it though life? I've seen them at their best and their worst. I know that growing up is tough, but: sometimes they make it really hard on themselves.

At certain times of the day during the school year, there can be up to a couple hundred Kids at the downtown Transfer Center waiting to catch the bus. It's like a powder keg just waiting to explode. This group of Kids is comprised of all Kids from all over the city. There is a gathering of age groups and ethnic groups in a confined area so the risk of conflicts between or amongst the groups is common. Most of the time the conflicts are minor, but; there have been some big fights down at the Transfer Center where Police intervention was needed.

One afternoon as I waited at the Transfer Center for the other buses to arrive, I witnessed something that was unbelievable. I watched as two young girls stole a pack of cigarettes from a challenged elderly man. I recognized both the man and the two girls as beings customers of our Transit System. The elderly man was standing near the front of my bus so I had a good view of what went down. This is what happened. The two girls approached the man and started flirty with him. Being a guy he played along with their flirtatious games. The one girl stood behind the guy and started rubbing the guys back and talking to him. Meanwhile the other girl stood in front of the guy talking to him and using body language to keep his attention. You know how girls act when their flirting when they're up to no good. The girl standing in front of the man unbuttoned a couple buttons on her blouse and was showing a little skin to him. When I say a little skin; I mean a little. There wasn't, in my opinion much to see and beside she was just a kid, but; the guy was enjoying the attention and the show that the girls were putting on for him.

Nobody in the immediate vicinity paid any attention to what the girls were doing because there were just a lot of people standing around. I thought to myself something's not right here. I kept watching to see what those two girls were really up to. After the girls felt that they had complete control over this guy, they put their plan into action. I watched as the girl that was rubbing the guys back; started rubbing the guy's shoulders, arms and sides. She had her hands roaming all over this guy and he was just taking it all in. As good as I could tell the girl did not touch his privates or his buttock area, but; everyplace else on him seemed to be fair game.

I watched as the girl that was standing in back of the guy; take her left hand and reach around into the guys left side coat pocket. The guy didn't notice because he was just enjoying all the attention. The girl that was standing in front of the guy kept his attention by talking to him. I watched as the one girl took a pack of cigarettes out of the guys coat pocket and then put the package of cigarettes into her pocket. There was a green rubber band or ribbon wrapped around the cigarette package so I really couldn't tell what kind they were, but; I knew that they were cigarettes.

After they accomplished stealing the guy's cigarettes, the girls just walked away from the guy. As they were walking away they both waved and threw the guy kisses. He was satisfied, but; didn't have a clue that the girls took his smokes. The two girls performed well together and it seemed like they had used this ruse before. As the girls walked away; they were laughing and joking among themselves. Mission accomplished.

The guy walked over to one of the other buses and boarded it. It was kind of funny because as I looked around the Transfer Center and it was virtually empty. All of the people that were milling around had gotten on the buses. That left just a handful of people waiting around. I was mad because there was nothing that I could do about what those girls pulled. I figured that they'll get theirs one day.

A few days later, guess who should board my bus, but; one of the girls who had stole the cigarettes and a woman that I believed to be her mother. As they got on the bus I greeted them both with a very audacious "Good morning!"

With the girl's mom standing by her side, I said to the girl in a sarcastic manner, "Hey, did you tell your mom what you and your girlfriend did the other day." The girl gave me funny looks like what are you talking about?

As the girl was walking toward the rear of the bus, she turned away from me and said, "Come on Mom, I have no idea what he's talking about."

The Mom sat down in the front seat of the bus and looked at me with a look of disgust on her face and said. "Is there something going on that I should know about?"

I said, "Yes."

By now the girl had come back to the front of the bus and sat down beside her mother. The girl had a worried look on her face. She didn't have a clue to what I was going to say. She said in a very snippy attitude, "What's so important that you gotta tell my Mom?"

I said to the girl, "I was at the Transfer Center the other day and I watched as you and that other girl stole the cigarettes out of that challenged man's coat pocket. I don't know what kind of cigarettes they were, but: I can tell you that the package had a green ribbon or tape around it."

The Mom asked, "What did this other girl look like?"

I said," She is a very skinny tall girl with long hair. She also had on a jacket that was kind of unique. It was orange and had some kind of dog picture on it."

The Mom looked at the girl and said, "That sounds a lot like your friend. I don't remember her name, but; she is the one that you always get off the bus with when you get home."

The girl just sat there staring at me. She was fuming. I figured since she was mad at me anyways, I should keep going, so; I said, "I think I saw your daughter put that pack of cigarettes into her inside coat pocket."

The Mom looked at the girl and very sternly said, "Open your coat and take everything out of your inside coat pocket, now!" The girl hesitated for a moment and then complied with her Mom's request. The contents that she took out of her pocket, besides all kind of girly stuff, included a pack of cigarettes with a green piece of duct tape wrapped around it. Why the duct tape was wrapped around the cigarette package; I haven't a clue.

The Mom gave the girl a stern look that showed her dissatisfaction with the entire incident at hand and said to the girl, "We'll deal with this when we get home."

The Mom turned to me and in a very apologetic tone said, "Thank you very much sir. I can assure you that my daughter will never do anything like that again." She turned and looked at her daughter and her daughter just sat there looking out the bus window. She knew that her mom meant what she said.

I replied to the lady, "No problem and continued with my route."

I see that young lady now and then at the bus Transit Center. I have never again seen her with her tall skinny friend, nor; have I ever seen her doing anything wrong. She behaves like a young lady now. On the occasions when she was riding on my bus, she was very cordial and friendly. I never brought that bus ride with her mom up again. I figured she learned her lesson and mom had taken care of it. I really wish that more Moms' and Dads' would get involved with their Kids like that mom did. I don't know and really don't care how she handled the situation, but; whatever she did it worked.

Chapter 9

THE CONTEST

It never surprises me to the things that Kids will come up with to pass the time while they're on the bus. There is always one in the group that will think of a game that they can play on the bus. Most of these games are simple and fun, but; occasionally they come up with one that they regret playing. If the game is too loud or bothering the other Passenger, that is where the Bus Driver steps in. The Kids know how far they can push their luck with the Bus Driver and they usually push it right to the limit. All the Drivers know this and they all react differently to stop the Kid's shenanigans.

I remember a Saturday morning a while back when three Kids about eleven or twelve years old boarded my bus. The all asked me politely if I could drop them off at the YMCA. They all were carrying backpacks with what I assumed extra clothes and gym shoes. All the boys were in a good mood and there was a lot of trash talk going on between them about the upcoming basketball game that they were going to. It was nothing out of the ordinary that the Kids did to physic out their opponents. My route took me right past their destination. I recognized these boys from previous trips that they had taken. They never caused any problems on the bus, but; occasionally they had to be asked to tone it down. When these boys would go out on these weekend ventures, they would always sit in the front of the bus so that they could look out of the front windshield as we drove along. They thought that it was cool. I didn't care where they sat as long as they behaved themselves.

While we were driving the route one of the boys burped. He tried to cover the burp with his hand, but; he reacted too slowly and the burp came out unexpectedly. The two other boys started to laugh. While they were laughing; the boy who had burped originally, burped out load again. This time he let it go full force. The burp was loud and long and the other two Kids started laughing louder. About that time one of the boys that had been laughing made a burp himself. Let the games begin. I sat there just driving, watching and listening. The one kid burped the entire alphabet, while; the other kid was burping out some song that I couldn't recognize. The third kid was trying to burp, but; he was having problems.

The first and second boy was now facing one another and burping toward one another. I thought of it as a burping face-off. They would make gurgitations within their little throats and then let out some loud burps. The two boys had their game faces on and were trying their best to out burp the other. The third boy just sat there in amazement as his two friends were competing against one another. He didn't even try to compete with them; he just sat there watching them burp.

After about a minute of both of the Kids burping continuously, they both took a little break. During the break, they were asking each other how they were making the burps. Kind of sharing techniques I guess. After the brief conversation and pause; the boys tried out the new burping techniques that they had just learned from each other. It was all going quite well until one of the boys in the burping contest passed gas while he was laughing at his counter part. I heard the flatulent and I was seated about four feet away from him. The flatulent was loud and must have had been odiferous because all three Kids started laughing uncontrollably and holding their nose. That is when one of the boys came up with the idea to have a flatulent contest.

I'm driving the bus and just listening to their little remarks. Nobody else was on board so I figured what could it hurt, beside; I was getting a good laugh out of their antics myself. I was hoping that they didn't need a judge because I was the only one available and I had already made up my mind that I was going to decline if asked. Besides somebody had to be the grownup, so I figure that why not me. Beside I was driving the bus.

All three of the boys sat there discussing the rules of the contest. They came up with two rule and three categories. The first rule was that they would take turns at making the flatulence with the oldest boy going first and the youngest going last. The second rule was that the other two boys couldn't bother the one trying to flatulent. The contest would be divided into the categories. The categories were loudness, longevity and odor. I'm just hoping that the contest gets underway before we get to their destination. I guess it's a guy thing, I don't know. I think rules are dumb, but; in any contest you need them.

It was the first kid's turn and he produced a flatulent almost immediately. I was astounded at how fast it happened. He started bragging to his friends on how good he was and that they didn't have a chance to beat him. Then it dawned on me that he was the one that had come up with the idea of having the flatulent contest in the first place. I think that he knew something that the other contestants didn't know.

It was now the second Kids turn. I watched in the mirror as the young man tried his best to pass some gas. The faces that he was making were hilarious. He was also shifting his body as if he were trying to find a comfortable way to sit. Nothing worked for him. After a minute or two he told the other boys that he couldn't do it and would have to pass his turn. The first boy was beaming and gloating. He made some comments to the last contestant on how he was going to lose. It was now the last boys turn.

The last boy sat there not saying a word. He didn't make faces like the other boys did; he just sat there with his eyes closed and with no emotions showing on his face. He was concentrating big time. I drove the bus and glanced back at him occasionally. After a few seconds he produced a small flatulent. It was loud, not too long and I couldn't tell you if it was malodorous or not. But; it was definitely passed gas. I think that it surprised him as much as it surprised the other contestants.

The first boy made some comment to the third contestant about the quality of what was produced and said, "I can beat that easy." Meanwhile, the second contestant just sat there in awe and I sure that he was wondering, as I was, how did they do it? In the past I tried to produce gas at will and couldn't, must be a new breed of Kids I guess. It was now the first contestants turn to beat the third contestants bid. The bus was almost at their destination and I, for whatever reasons, wanted to see the outcome of the contest.

The first contestant, not wanting to get beat by his buddies, was determined to produce the winning flatulent. I thought that he was taking the contest way too serious and seemed like he had to win at any cost. In my opinion he had already won the contest. The young man very confidently stood up, bent at the hip and made an ugly face. He was concentrating on winning and wasn't about to give up. It's that guy thing again. What happened next was as much as a surprise to him as it was to me. As he was trying to flatulent he said, "OOPS!" The other two boys had forgotten about the contest by now because we were pulling up to the YMCA and they were excited about getting there.

The boy that had said, "OOPS", had passed a flatulent that was loud, long and very noisy. If I had been the judge, he would have won hands down with what he produced. The look on the boys face went from concentration to pure terror. He looked at my reflection in the mirror and he knew that I knew exactly what had happened. I didn't say anything; I just sat there watching him. I was thinking to myself, "I hope that he doesn't get that stuff on the floor or the seats." What a considerate and compassionate guy I am, huh.

I was happy because I was pulling the bus over to the curb in front of the YMCA. I know that the other two boys didn't realize what had happened. When the bus came to a complete stop; they got up, grabbed their back-packs and exited the bus. The first contestant walked to the exit very slowly and turned to me and said, "Sure is a good thing that I brought extra clothes with me today."

I said to him, "Too bad that there wasn't a category for biggest mess, huh? I know that you would have won that one too."

He just gave me a dirty look and waddled away toward the gym door. From that day on, I don't allow the Kids on my bus to have any contests that I feel could accidentally make any kind of mess with body fluids. That too, is a guy thing!

Chapter 10

I'm a Step-Mom

Sometime we assume too much and take things for granted. It is not fair to judge those that are challenged and are trying to cope with everyday life situations. Some people are learning as they go. I know at times that I fall into that category. A few years ago I was driving the bus on the Friday before a long three day holiday weekend. I'm thinking that it was Labor Day weekend, but; it doesn't matter. Well anyways, the bus was crowded as Passengers were trying to deal with the dilemma of working before the holiday. Spirits were high and most conversations on the bus that day centered on what people were going to be doing for the weekend.

Two Dental technicians were seated to my right and they were sharing opinions with each other about family gatherings. These two technicians have used our Transit System regularly, Monday through Friday, for the last couple of years. On the second bus run of the day you can count on them being on the bus. They both have very pleasant personalities and pretty much keep to themselves. I have noticed that when they do talk amongst themselves about the other Passengers, they do it in a secretive manner as not to offend anyone. Hey whatever, they're not doing anything else that anybody else isn't doing, but; they use good discretion.

On that morning the dental technicians were talking about their Step-children and how they looked forward to seeing them for the holiday. They were laughing and carrying on about how some of their relatives accepted their stepchildren and others didn't. That is when one of the technicians said, "I really enjoy being a Mom to those Kids, even though; I'm their Step-Mom."

About that time a lady who was sitting across the aisle from the technicians very seriously said, "What's a Step-Mom?" The lady who had asked the question is an adult, but; is mentally challenged. She is married to a man who is quite a bit older than she is and he is retired. This is a great example of when people say that everyone has a soul mate out there somewhere. I don't know, and actually don't care, what their circumstances are. All I know is that they're in love, they're happy and he treats her like a queen.

I do know that her husband has a couple of children from a previous marriage and that they are older. I know this to be true because he told me that he was widowed and raised the Kids by himself. He also told me that he never thought that he would marry again, but; he was wrong and things change.

One of the Technicians said to the lady, "You don't know what a Step-Mother is?"

With a quizzical look on her face, the lady said, "No. Could you please tell me?"

"You're a Step mother if the man that you married has children from a previous marriage," the technician explained.

The lady very seriously said, "You mean that if my husband has children, then I'm their Step-mother?"

The technician responded with a puzzled, "Yes."

The lady who had been talking to the technicians started crying and talking to her self out loud and saying, "I'm a Step Mom! I'm a Step Mom!" She was very happy of the news and it seemed like nobody had ever told her, or she never figured it out, that she indeed was a Step-mom.

I sat there driving the bus thinking that this was good for the lady. She was happy because she was a Step-mom and it was good to see her smiling. When she usually rides the bus she doesn't regularly have a smile on her face. Well everybody on the bus caught on by now that she had good news. This was not because all the other Passengers heard or even cared about her conversation with the technicians, but rather; the lady went through the entire bus telling the other Passengers the good news that she had just found out. She was ecstatic! Most of the other Passengers congratulated her with salutations and high fives. The

Passengers that didn't really know her mostly said "good for you" and went on with their business.

After a few minutes the lady came back and sat down next to the Technicians and said, "Thank you for making me happy!"

The Technician just shook her head in amazement. After a few seconds the technician asked the lady, "How long have you been married?"

The lady answered, "About two years."

Technician replied, "You've been married two years and nobody told you that those were your Step Kids?"

"I didn't think of it that way. I had some suspicions at Christmas when some of the gifts that they gave me had S-MOM on them, but; they are always joking with me so I thought that it was a joke. Now I know that it wasn't and I'm a Step-Mom!" The remainder of that bus ride went fast. Passengers were disembarking as we reached their destinations. The next thing I knew, I was the only one on the bus. I kind of appreciated the silence for a little while.

For the next two months every time the lady who had found out that she was a Step-Mom boarded my bus; she would enter the bus and say her name followed by, "I'm a Step Mom." The first fifteen or so times that she identified herself in this manner it was kind of funny, but: after that many times it really started to become annoying. I was happy for her, but; I really wished that she would knock it off. After about six months she was still happy and talking about it. Awe, maybe I should just let it go and let her enjoy it, after all; she has been a Step-Mom for over two years and has some lost time to make up.

Chapter 11

THE MOONSHINE STILL

I met this one fellow on the bus who was born and raised on top of a mountain in eastern Kentucky. He told me that his family has lived on and owned that mountain for the last one hundred and fifty years. He is temporary living up here in southern Wisconsin to work at a nearby power plant. When he is not working at the power plant he rides the bus for fun. He said that when he is back home, that there are no buses for him to ride. He also claims that it is the cheapest way to kill time, besides hunting and fishing, that he ever seen. My friend loves to talk and has a deep Kentucky accent. I asked him what his name was and he told me to call him "King of the Mountain." I said, "OK. Whatever."

My friend has told me quite a bit about himself. He is a definite talker. When he is on the bus he is either asking me questions about whatever or he's telling me a story. I drive the bus and he does all the talking. He is constantly looking around or doing something. He is really hyper. When he starts to become a distraction to my driving, I just tune him out. All guys have the ability of selective hearing. If you don't believe me, just ask my wife.

One day while he was on the bus a group of people got on who were talking about how to conserve energy. They were coming up with all these elaborate ideas on the different fossil fuels and alternate energy plans. The groups discussion turned toward ethanol based fuels. I was watching in the mirror as they were talking amongst themselves. My friend, "The King of the Mountain", was sitting in the front seat of the bus to my right and not saying a word. I thought this to be rather odd. I know that he wanted to join in their conversation, but; for some reason he didn't.

When the group started talking about corn based alcohol, the term moonshine came up. I watched as my friend sat there, not saying a word, yet; clinging to everything that they were saying about moonshine. One girl in the group said, "What the heck is moonshine?"

One fellow from the group who seemed to know everything about everything says, "Moonshine is booze that they make down south in the mountains. I'm sure you seen those movies where those Country Bumpkins that live way back in the mountains have illegal stills and make booze. Moonshine is made from potatoes or corn and supposedly it is a high grain alcohol. I don't believe all those stories that I've heard about it."

The girl said. "What kind of stories." Everybody on the bus was now listening to this expert on moonshine. I watched as my friend just sat there. I was expecting an argument or at least a few comments from him based on some of the stories that he had told me. I'm sure that my Kentucky friend was a little bit ticked when the fellow talking made that comment about Country Bumpkins.

Responding to the girl's question, the know it all guy said, "Moonshine is supposed to be like a medicine, but; at the same time be rated over two hundred and fifty proof of alcohol. Some people say that you can use it like a cleaning fluid and at the same time enjoy drinking it for pleasure. I find that hard to believe. Who in their right mind would even think of something like that? There is no way that anybody could make something that strong, let alone, think about using it as a fuel alternative. Moonshine is just a waste of time. Our government needs to find some alternate form of energy to get us less oil dependant of other countries."

The group's conversation came to an abrupt stop when one of the group's members pulled the chime line indicating to me that they were at their destination and wanted off the bus. I pulled the bus over to the curb and let them off at the next stop. My friend just sat there not saying a word, but; the look on his face told me that he had a lot to say. He had a look on his face as if he were the cat that caught the canary. After the group of people got off the bus; "The King of the Mountain" and I were the only ones on the bus again.

After I merged the bus back into traffic I said to my friend, "I thought that you told me that your Daddy had ran a moonshine still?"

My friend shook his head and looked at me and laughed. After a little bit he said to me,"Yea, my Daddy got a still. He got himself a mighty fine still. I had a good laugh at that guy telling them others about moonshine. He was right about a couple things, moonshine is a medicine and it can be used for a cleaning fluid from the same jar. I really didn't like his Country Bumpkin comment. If my brother or my cousin would have heard it they would have had words with that guy. My Momma and Daddy raised me to be a God faring man and I just minded my own when he was making his little comments. He sure enough was wrong in saying that moonshine can't be used as fuel though."

I said,"What do yaw all mean? (Did yaw all notice that all of a sudden I'm talking with a deep southern accent? What ever!) Why didn't you say something about your daddy's moonshine?"

He said to me," There is something's that you just don't brag about. You know; Revenuers. Let me tell you something. A couple years ago we had some financial troubles and we had to do thing to make ends meet. Gasoline was a couple pennies shy of five bucks a gallon and we needed to use our old tractor to do farm chores. We actually ran that tractor for two seasons on moonshine rather than gasoline. Yea, there was some major maintenance on the tractor because of us using the shine, but; we did all the work ourselves in the barn and saved us a lot of money. More important we kept the farm a running."

Well after about six months, my friend finished his job up here at the power plant and moved back to Kentucky. I don't remember the name of the little town that my friend lives near, nor; do I know exactly where that mountain is that he lives on. I think that I conveniently forgot all that information just in case I run into any Revenue Men. I was thinking that just maybe it would be in our countries best interests if some of our politicians went back up in them mountains and learned some of the things that the people who live down there know. I'm sure some things could get done a lot cheaper and faster with the input from the people who live down there. But then again yaw all, what do I know: I just drive the bus.

Chapter 12

HOW ARE YOU TODAY?

If you want to be a Bus Driver, it is best if you're a "People Person." I say this because if you're a "People Person" it makes your job seem a lot easier and the days go by faster. In my opinion, a "People Person" is an individual who enjoys being around people, but; can communicate well with everyone without actually saying a word. It's kind of like being married. You know what I'm talking about. A great example would be if your better half is talking to you and you're watching your favorite television program; that's truly multitasking as far as I'm concerned. If you're good at it, mind you it does take some practice, you can keep two completely different entities happy. First and foremost you keep your better half happy by actually giving the impression that your paying attention to her ramblings about something that you're not interested in. Secondly you're keeping yourself happy by enjoying your television program. See where I'm going here? A "People Person" is flexible and rolls with the flow by not letting insignificant incidents ruin their day.

An elderly woman gets on my bus one day and I welcome her on the bus by saying, "Good morning". This is something that I say to all my Passengers in the morning is nothing out of the ordinary.

She acknowledged me back and said, "Good morning to you young man and how are you doing this fine day."

To which I replied, "I'm doing fine. How are you today?" Everything sounds normal up until now right? This was just two individuals making small talk and trying to make it through the day. When people ask "How are you today?" they usually say it to be nice and not they're trying to be nosey. This is just a simple rhetorical question; that's all.

The elderly woman got on the bus and was in the process of sitting down in the front seat on the bus to my right. She started talking about "How she was doing" even before she set her bags down on the seat. She continued to talk and tell me "How she was doing today" for her entire bus ride. I picked this Passenger up near the downtown area and she was going to the far end of my route. This was about a twenty minute bus ride, but; this time the ride seemed like an eternity.

She started talking to me about her health. She told me that she had a Doctor's appointment last week and the doctor wanted to do some tests, but; she didn't want that doctor to do the tests because her friend told her that that doctor didn't perform the tests well on her. Sounds confusing huh? You should have been there. Well she continued on how those tests were to expensive and that nobody in her family has ever had that problem so she couldn't figure out why the doctors thought that she would have that problem. She wanted to bring her daughter with her to her next doctor appointment, but: her daughter was going on vacation and couldn't make it. I though that the lady was going to ask me to go with her to her doctor's appointment. She didn't, thank God.

She was rambling on about how her back hurt and how she had a bunion on her left foot that was starting to become a bother when she was walking. Speaking of walking, that is when she told me that she didn't like to walk no more because she was afraid of all the crime and violence that was going on. I sat there listening and driving the bus. Yea, if they handed out gold medals for talking this woman would have a room full. About that time, my Dispatcher called and I answered with my radio. I was stopped at a red light so I could talk safely because the bus wasn't moving. The lady still kept talking to me as I spoke with my Dispatcher on the radio. I shut the woman's voice out and tried to listen to my Dispatcher's request. The request was about an upcoming transfer. Have you ever tried to carry two conversations on and not being the one doing any of the talking?

The lady was just warming up. She started telling me about what she had for breakfast, what she was going to have for lunch and what she needed to buy so she could make supper. She told me that she couldn't eat a lot of starchy or salty food and that tomatoes gave her canker sores. She takes care of the canker sores by rinsing her mouth out with hot salty water. She told me that it kind of stings a little bit, but; it takes care of the canker sores. Did you know that canker sores run in her family and that her grandfather almost died from them? It was a good thing for him that his wife, the bus rider's step- grandmother was a nurse and took care of him. Incidentally, her grandparents met at a local baseball game; in the third inning; at the concession stand and fell madly in love with each other. It was love at fist sight for them. Her grandfather's favorite team, while we're on the subject, won the baseball game. We drove on.

I glanced at my watch and realized that I had at least five more minutes to endure. It was kind of like being in the twilight zone and I was expecting to pick up Rod Stieger at the next stop. He wasn't there, but; a large group of Kids were. As the ten or so Kids boarded the bus the lady continued talking. The Kids were talking amongst themselves and didn't pay any attention to what the lady had to say. If they did notice, they didn't give any indication of it.

The lady started telling me about her sister's son, her nephew, and that he was getting out of jail. She said that she didn't trust him as far as she could throw him. Did you know that she used to run on the track team when she was in high school? The lady continued talking about her family and their problems. She didn't want to go into depth on this topic because her nephew was breaking her sister's heart and she didn't like to talk about family matters.

I knew that this torment was going to end because I had just a few blocks to go. Technically I wasn't talking to her, I was driving the bus. I was just trying to be nice. I guess if you consider the grunts and sounds that I was making; then theoretically I was involved the conversation, but; that's as far as it went. It was like having a radio on with one station at one volume. I could see the end in sight.

As I pulled the bus up to the last stop on the route, the lady stopped talking. I turned to make sure that she didn't pass out from lack of oxygen from talking too much. She was fine. I opened both the front and back doors of the bus and the other Passengers exited. It took the elderly woman a minute or so to gather all of her belongings. I waited patiently.

As she was exiting the bus through the front door; she stopped and turned toward me and said, "That was such a pleasant conversation we had, we'll have to do that more often. Have a nice day. Bye."

I sat there listening to her for twenty minutes straight, while; she spoke nonstop. I wanted to make sure that if I did say anything to her that I wouldn't say anything to make her start talking again. My response to her was, "Please watch your step and have a nice day." I waited for her response; there wasn't one, thank God! The lady got off the bus and started to slowly walk away. As she was walking away from the bus another lady approached her from out of nowhere and asked her, "How are you doing?" When I heard that comment; I closed the bus door and proceeded to drive away from the ladies as fast and as safely as I possibly could. I didn't want to get involved. I really didn't want to hear what the answer was going to be. In a way I felt sorry for the lady that asked the question, but; I got over it really quickly.

That bus ride has taught me a valuable lesson. I still greet my Passengers in a cheerful manner regardless of what time of day it is. The only thing that I do different now is that I'm very careful when I ask the question "How are you today?"

Chapter 13

THE HOSPITAL GOWN

The first thought that came to my mind was; "Unbelievable." I was on the first run of the day and if this was an indication of how the rest of the day was going to be; I should have just gone home right then and there. I was pulling the bus up to a bus shelter that was located in a residential neighborhood on the outskirts of town. There in the bus-shelter sat a man dressed in a pair of black socks and a hospital gown. I opened the front door of the bus and the man got up from the bench and walked up to the bus. That is when I noticed that the man had a hospital wristband on his wrist and a blood tube attached to his right arm. I sat there watching in disbelief as the man walked up to the bus; I couldn't wait to hear what he had to say.

"Good morning", he cheerfully called out to me as he was walking up to the bus.

I responded with a, "Hey back at cha. What's up?"

Then the story started. "Well, I got into a little trouble last night with the guys at the bar and the next thing yaw know is I'm at the hospital. Well the cops showed up and said that they wanted to talk to me and I got mad and left, you know. I think I snuck out the back door or something. Well, I'm not exactly sure what happened next, but: here I am and all I want to do is go home now. I think that I fell asleep in this bus stop. I've been on the bus a lot of times and it never dawned on me that those benches in the bus shelters were so comfortable. So can yaw help me out?"

Not wanting to show him how much I didn't care, in a very inquisitive voice I answered, "How can I help you?"

He continued, "You see, I think I left my wallet and keys at the hospital and I know that sooner or later I'm going to have to go get them, but; I want to go home first and take a shower and clean up a bit. You see what I'm saying?"

"Not really", I replied.

"Well yaw see, I think that the cops want to put me in jail and I don't want to go there dressed like this. Have you ever been in jail?" He exclaimed.

Not wanting to get this guy upset or more importantly, not wanting to become an accomplice by harboring a fugitive to justice; I figured that I'd play ignorant. That's something I'm good at. I immediately answered, "No! That still doesn't answer my question. How do you want me to help you?"

So he stopped beating around the bush and said, "Can yaw give me a ride home? When we get there I'll give you ten bucks for your trouble. OK?" He then started to walk up the front entrance of the bus.

I put my hand up and responded to him by saying, "Man I can't do that. I don't want to get fired. I'll tell you what I can do for you; I'll contact my Dispatcher and he'll send someone over to pick you up. OK?"

"Ya, that will be OK I guess," he said with a frustrated voice. He stepped off the bus and turned to go back toward the bus shelter.

"Hey, I got a newspaper here if you want something to read until your ride shows up" I suggested to him. By now all I wanted to do is get out of there, but; I figured if he had something to do that he would be more apt to stay put and his ride will find him faster.

I pulled the bus away from the shelter and called my Dispatcher. I told them about my encounter with the man dressed in a hospital gown at the bus shelter. I also told them that the guy was sitting in the bus shelter reading the newspaper and if Dispatch was going to call anyone that he should do it now. I emphasized the word "NOW" so that Dispatch would understand the urgency of the situation. The Dispatcher responded with, "I understand and I'll take care of it immediately!" and he broke off from our conversation.

I drove on with my route. I was about three blocks away from the bus shelter from where I had left the guy when I turned onto a busy roadway. I had driven about a block on the roadway when I encountered three Police vehicles headed back toward the bus shelter that I had just left earlier. All three squads had there mars lights on, their sirens were screaming and they were traveling exceptionally fast. Shortly behind the Police cars was an ambulance that seemed to be following them.

I don't know exactly what happened back at that bus shelter that morning; because, I never read anything in the local newspaper about the incident and my Dispatcher never heard anything back from whomever he called. All I do know is when I drove past that bus shelter, about an hour later; there was no activity around it. All I saw was a: empty bus shelter, a folded newspaper on the bench in the bus shelter and a discarded hospital gown on the floor of the bus shelter. If I thought that it was "Unbelievable" when I first saw the guy in the bus shelter; I can't imagine what the Police and Ambulance Personnel thought when they first saw him. But after thinking about it for a moment; it probably wasn't that bad because the guy did have a pair of black socks on.

Chapter 14

THE MAN ON BICYCLE

Life is short and we never know when our time on earth will come to an end. I think about those words every time I recall this next story. It was a very pleasant early spring day and everybody was enjoying the mild temperatures. People were out walking, riding bikes or just surveying their yards after the long winter. Kids were out playing in their yards and mom and dads were again sitting on their porches enjoying the pleasant weather. It was kind of like everybody had come out of hibernation because of being cooped up in the house all winter long.

I was driving an afternoon route that day and traffic was extremely heavy and the streets were quite congested with all kinds of traffic. As I pulled the bus into a busy strip mall that was on the end of my route, I was looking forward to my short layover there. At the strip mall I knew that I could park the bus and get out of the Drivers seat and stretch my legs. A well deserved break if I don't say so myself.

I glanced at my watch and the time was three twenty-seven P.M. I said to myself in a very smug way, "Right on time." As I slowly maneuvered the bus through the main thorough way of the parking lot, I encountered a man riding a bicycle. The man was riding his bike very cautiously and was enjoying his day. He was riding his bike and smiling as if he hadn't a care in the world. I noticed that the man on the bike had taken the utmost precautions just in case he had a spill off the bike. The bike looked as if it was brand new or perhaps it was one that had been taken care of. Any how, it looked to be in excellent condition. He was wearing a red safety helmet and had knee and elbow guards on that matched the helmet. I said to myself, "Hey, yaw gotta do, what yaw gotta do."

As I drove past the man he smiled at me and nodded his head at me. I in turn smiled and nodded back to him. Nice guy I thought to myself. That got me to thinking that maybe I should get my wife's bike and my bike out and we should go for a bike ride since the weather was so nice. Well I parked the bus at the bus stop in the strip mall and I had time to get out of the Drivers seat for a few minutes. I've learned that when I'm working and I do have opportunities to park the bus and get little breaks from driving that I try to focus on not wanting to be at home because it just makes the day go longer. So I guess that I kind of just vegetate while I'm waiting to continue my route.

Time pasted quickly and it was time to continue my route. I glanced at my watch and the time was three thirty five P.M. I got in the bus and resumed my route. As I was pulling out of the plaza, traffic was starting to back up due to a commotion further down the block. I pulled into traffic and waited to continue. Since it was such a nice day outside I had my Drivers window open, I could hear in the distance the wail of emergency vehicles. Traffic was now at a standstill. Up ahead at the stop and go lights there was some kind of activity going on, but; I didn't know what. I watched as numerous Police and emergency vehicles converged and stopped about one block ahead of me. I could see from my lofty vantage point on the bus that Police officers were taking charge of the traffic situation and emergency paramedics were taking care of something else.

The traffic started moving along pretty fast because of law enforcement intervention. As I drove the bus through the intersection where all the emergency vehicles were, I saw a man being worked on by paramedics. I recognized the man as the man that I saw on the bicycle at the plaza from his red knee pads and red elbow pads. His red bicycle helmet was on the ground next to him. He was laying on the ground next to his mangled bicycle. He had been hit by a car. The car that hit the bicyclist was parked about ten feet away from where the paramedic's were working on the bicyclist. Police officers were talking to a distraught young man who obviously had been driving the car. I glanced at my watch and the time was three forty two P.M.

I was upset the rest of the day thinking about the bicyclist that had got hit by the car. I thought about how he was enjoying himself and how he had smiled and nodded to me. That night I had trouble sleeping thinking about what I had seen. The next morning on the front page of the local paper I read an article about a man on a bicycle being killed instantly after being struck by a car. There was a picture of the accident victim and I immediately recognized the man. The article also stated that the Driver of the car that hit the bicyclist was ticketed for inattentive driving. It was the same accident that I saw the day before.

I didn't know the man, but; just knowing what I saw made me extremely depressed. It's amazing how in less than fifteen minutes a person's life can be taken. One minute you're riding your bike enjoying yourself and the next minute you're laying on the ground fighting for your life. I think about the man's family a lot. I also hope that the young man that was driving the car is coping with the burden that was placed on him. Since that tragic day, I now make a point of telling my love one's how much I love them every chance that I get. You never know what life has got in store for you.

Chapter 15

MAN VS. BUS

Some people at times don't have any kind of civil decency when they ride the bus. I find this to be true, particularly when individuals have consumed too much alcohol or have been experimenting with illegal drugs or whatever. One evening a man in his mid twenties to early thirties got on my bus and it was obvious to me that this person was either drunk or stoned. Could have been a combination of both, I really don't know nor do I care. All I do know is that this individual was acting the fool from the time that he stepped on the bus until the time that he got off.

After boarding the bus this individual started talking on his cell phone rather loud and using vulgar and profane language to whomever he was talking to. There was en elderly couple on the bus who he made a rather obscene comment to when the elderly man asked him if he would not use the Lord's name in vain.

After he made the comment to the elderly man I interjected and told the guy to clean up his act or he could get off the bus. He did not like my comment and gave me a dirty look. I told him that if he wanted to stay on the bus the he needed to keep his conversation down and not to be bothering the other Passengers. He knew that I meant it.

After we drove a couple blocks the elderly couple got off at their normal bus stop. I paid attention to the fellow that made a comment to them to make sure that he wasn't going to follow them off the bus and give them a hard time. He just sat there so I figured that the incident was over. About twelve blocks down, the chime line sounded. I had one Passenger on the bus so I knew exactly who had pulled the cord. My inebriated Passenger got up from his seat and walked to the front of the bus. I kept an eye on him because I didn't really trust him because of his condition. He walked to the front of the bus and started down the front stairwell. When he got half way down the stairwell he stopped and turned toward me. I really kept an eye on him now and was prepared to defend myself if I needed to. I just sat there in the Drivers seat, waiting.

The man started yelling and cursing at me. I've been in this position on numerous occasions and know that the best thing for me to do is to not argue or try to reason with individuals like this. If I let him vent, he will feel like he won and just go away. Nope, not this guy. He got off the bus and ran to the front of the bus and started spitting at the bus. He was spitting on the front windshield and standing right in front of the bus. I closed the bus door and just sat there. I couldn't take the chance of hitting him with the bus by trying to drive away so I just sat there with the bus idling.

Every time the fellow would spit at the bus; I would turn the wipers on and activate the windshield washer. After about three minutes of this little game I called my Dispatcher. The conversation went like this.

Me, "This is bus 3501 and I have an inebriated individual standing in front of my bus and he is spitting at my windshield. Just letting you know this is causing me to run behind schedule."

Dispatcher, "Bus 3501 just drive around him and resume your route."

Me, "Like I said, this guy is standing in front of the bus and I cannot move the bus. Could you please call the Police for assistance?"

Dispatcher, "Is this guy hurting you or damaging the bus?"

Me, "Well he's not hurting me, but; he is standing in front of the bus spitting at the windshield."

Dispatcher, "I'm not contacting the Police. When he gets done spitting at the bus, resume your route. Keep me posted"

Me, "10-4."

The fellow continued to spit at the bus for the next five minutes or so. I knew that I had a full container of windshield wash under the hood so I was set for a while. He on the other hand started running low on spit. I say this because his spitting assault was starting to slow down.

After a few minutes more I contacted Dispatch again.

Me, "This is bus 3501, the guy is still standing in front of the bus spitting at it. What do you want me to do?"

Dispatch, "Are you still at the same location that you contacted me from earlier? Is that guy still spitting at your Bus?"

I responded, "Yes and yes."

Dispatcher, "You need to get going on your route immediately. What's the hold up?"

Me," Like I told you earlier. This guy is standing in front of my bus spitting at it. Could you please contact the Police?

Dispatcher, "No I'm not calling the Police."

Me, "Why not?"

Dispatcher, "Because you should be handling that predicament yourself."

Me, "How should I be handling it?"

Dispatcher, "You should just drive away!"

Me, "I can't because he is standing in front of the bus and won't move." About that time the guy that was spitting at the bus decided that enough was enough and started to walk away from the bus. As he was leaving, he kicked the bike rack that is located on the front of the bus. When he kicked the rack he must have hurt his leg, because he walked away with a pronounced lip. It was then that I said, "Dispatch the fellow that was spitting at the bus is walking away. Before he left he kicked the bike rack on front of the bus. I think that he hurt his leg when he kicked the rack. I am continuing with my route. 10-4?"

Dispatch, "Does the man that kicked the bicycle rack need medical assistance?"

Me, "Not that I can tell. He's is running away and I'm resuming my route."

Dispatcher, "Should I send an ambulance out to your location?"

Me, "Let me get this straight. I called and asked for Police assistance and you didn't feel that I needed help. Then this guy, who is now gone, bumps his leg while trying to damage the bus and you want to send an ambulance out to help him? Am I correct in my Assumptions?"

Dispatcher," Do you need for me to contact the Police and an ambulance or not?"

Me, "Maybe ten minutes ago it would have been nice, but; now there is no problem as far as I'm concerned."

Dispatcher, "10-4 bus 3501. Call anytime I can help. Resume your route." I finished my route that day and I still have many questions on the way that that incident was handled, but; in reality I'm over it.

I'm still trying to figure out what my biggest obstacle was that evening. I question myself and ask if there was something that I could have done to handle that situation better. I think I handled it OK, but; the question is: "Was it the inebriated Passenger who was acting like a fool or was it the Dispatcher that hadn't a clue?" I'm not sure, all I know is that I've never seen that Passenger again; the Dispatcher I spoke to that night has since changed jobs and moved on to bigger and better things; and quite noticeably, the windshield on bus 3501 really glistens in the sunlight when the sun beams strike it just right.

Chapter 16

THE LOTTERY TICKET

Everybody that rides the bus have different backgrounds. Some feel that they are superior to other Passengers because of their education or social status. These Passengers are condescending and very careful not to associate with those whom they feel are beneath them. Every once in a while individuals like this learn that they really aren't as intelligent or above the others as they think that they are.

One individual who rides the bus daily is a mentally challenged adult and one of the nicest people that you will ever meet. This individual's appearance sets him out in a crowd. He is a very large man and reminds me of the main character in the Hemmingway novel "Of Mice and Men." This individual can be intimidating if you do not know him. His sister once told me that he has the mind of a twelve year old child.

One morning at a local coffee shop while I was getting coffee preparing to start the day; I witnessed an incident that I will always remember. The Passenger that I described in the above paragraph was buying scratch off lottery tickets from a lottery machine and scratching the tickets as fast as he could buy them. He must have purchased at least fifteen one dollar tickets. After scratching the tickets he would put the winning tickets in his pants pocket and the losing tickets in the trash can. I was just standing by the counter drinking my coffee and watching this guy scratch the tickets. I notice little things like that it's just a little quirk of mine. There was at least four other people standing in line getting coffee and I was just killing time waiting to go to work.

I watched as the guy that was scratching the lottery tickets started laughing and started doing what I figured was a little victory dance. He stopped scratching the remaining lottery tickets that he held in his hand

and went up to the service counter and asked the counter person if they could cash in his winning ticket. The counter person replied with, "I cannot cash any lottery tickets until seven o' clock." The counter person then pointed to a sign that was posted above the cash register that stated, "Lottery tickets can only be cashed between seven AM and nine PM. Sorry for any inconvenience." I glanced at my watch and it was only five forty five AM.

The man with the tickets said, "I wanna buy more tickets; could you please cash this one ticket it's worth one hundred dollars!"

The counter person again told the man that he couldn't cash the tickets now, but; he would be more than happy to cash all of his winning tickets, including the hundred dollar winning ticket, in at seven o' clock. About that time a fellow, who I know is an attorney, came up to the man with the winning tickets and said, "I'll give you fifty dollars cash for the ticket right now and you don't have to wait until seven o' clock. What do you say?" The attorney was standing in line getting coffee when he heard the conversation between the two men about the lottery tickets. The attorney is also a regular bus Passenger and knows full well that the man with the lottery tickets was mentally challenged.

The man with the tickets told the attorney, "That don't seem fair, ain't I losing fifty dollars?"

The attorney smugly answered, "No you're not losing any money. I'm just putting those fifty dollars in my bank account, so do you want to scratch tickets now or do you want to wait until seven o' clock?" Everybody in the coffee shop knew that the attorney was taking advantage of the man with the winning lottery ticket. The man with the ticket looked confused and really didn't know what to do. He would look at the ticket in his hand and then looked at the attorney. He knew that he shouldn't give up that winning ticket, but; he wanted to buy more scratch tickets. The man still had tickets in his other hand that he hadn't scratched, so; I not sure what the big deal on his part was.

The attorney said, "I need an answer right now! Yes or no; I need to get going and don't have time for this!"

The man, with the winning lottery ticket hesitantly said, "OK." The attorney immediately produced two twenty's and a ten that he had hidden in his hand. He gave the money to the man, took the winning ticket from the man and hastily turned to leave the coffee shop. As he was walking out of the coffee shop door he turned and smugly said, "Have a nice day." Everyone that was in that coffee shop knew what had just happened.

I had to get going to work. I took my coffee and left the coffee shop. I made up my mind that I was going to talk to the challenged man the first opportunity that I could when he was on the bus. As I was leaving the coffee shop, I saw the man that sold the winning ticket buying more scratch off lottery tickets from the machine. I thought to myself, as I'm sure everybody in the coffee shop did, man was that attorney a jerk for doing that. He'll get his one day. I believe in what goes around comes around.

A couple days went by and as fate should have it the attorney and the challenged man both happened to be on my bus at the same time. I was parked downtown at the Transfer Center and I was waiting for the half hour so that I could continue my route. When the challenged man got on the bus, the attorney looked up from his newspaper and cautiously watched as the challenged man took a seat directly across from him. The attorney nodded to the challenged individual and the man nodded back. After their brief salutations the attorney went back to reading his newspaper. The attorney must have felt that the challenged man had forgotten what he had done to him.

The challenged individual sat there for a few minutes and then said to me in a very cheerful voice, "Hey Marty, I got a ticket just like I had the other morning."

I replied to him, "Good for you. Did yaw get it out of the same lottery machine?"

"Yep", he happily replied. "As soon as seven o'clock comes around, I'm gonna go get some more scratch offs." I was looking in the mirror while I was talking to the man and I had a good view of the entire interior of the bus. I watched as the attorney put his paper down and turned to the challenged man and said, "Is that ticket just like the one I brought from you the other morning?"

The challenged man hesitantly replied, "Ya, it's the same kind."

The attorney sat there for a few seconds and said, "I'll give you fifty dollars cash for that ticket right now!"

The challenged man answered with, "I don't know. Something don't seem fair." The attorney reached into his suit coat pocket and took out his wallet. He opened the wallet and said "darn I don't have fifty dollars in cash. I just have three twenties." The attorney sat there pondering to himself for a few seconds and said, "Awe what the hell, I'll give you sixty dollars for that ticket."

The challenged man sat there looking at the lottery ticket; obviously thinking about the proposed offer. Meanwhile I'm sitting there thinking that this ain't gonna happen again. I said to the challenged man, "Do you really think that it's a good idea to sell that ticket?"

The challenged man replied sternly with, "Yes, cause I want to buy more scratch off lottery tickets!" I was watching the attorney in the mirror and could tell that he was satisfied with the challenged mans response. The attorney quickly gave the challenged man the three twenty dollar bills that he had in his hand. The challenged man took the money and said to the attorney, "Are you sure that you want to do this?"

To which the attorney snappily answered, "Yes, now give me that ticket!" The challenged man tentatively handed the ticket over to the attorney. The attorney had the look on his face like the cat that caught the canary. I was very disappointed in both of them. I think I was more disappointed in myself for not doing more to stop the transaction, but; everything happened so fast.

After a few seconds the attorney loudly said, "Hey, this isn't a winning ticket!" To which the challenged man answered, "I know it ain't. All I said to Marty was that the ticket was the same kind I had the other morning. I didn't say it was a winner."

The attorney emphatically said to the challenged man, "Give me my sixty dollars back right now!"

The challenged man sat there for a few seconds and said, "No! I think we're even now. You were the one that offered to by that stupid ticket and I didn't want to sell it, but you insisted, No returns!" Needless to say I was flabbergasted. I really couldn't believe what had just happened. The challenged man had made the attorney look like a fool and the attorney knew it. I guess the attorney's greed got the best of him. The attorney angrily got up from his seat and said a profane word to the challenged man. With his newspaper tucked under his arm and a look of disgust on his face, the attorney stormed toward the bus exit door. As the attorney was exiting the bus, the Challenged man said to him, "Have a nice day!"

The attorney got off the bus and I have never seen him on my bus or any other the bus again. No loss as far as I'm concerned. I'm sure that this is one story that he won't be telling to his peers at any social gatherings. Every once in a while I see things happen, but; not as bitter sweet as this event was. I guess it's safe to say, especially in this case, "What goes around always comes around." I think that the greedy fool got what he deserved and that he found out that he wasn't as smart as he thought that he was. I love it!!!

Chapter 17

🚌

$100 Bill

It's O.K to make mistakes; everybody does at one time or another. Problem arises when someone makes a mistake and then tries to blame others for their oversight. For instance, a guy gets on the bus one morning and puts his money in the fare box. I did not notice anything unusual or out of the ordinary about that; it's what Passengers do when they get on the bus, it's called paying your fare.

I was busy punching daily transfers and wasn't really paying that much attention to what was going on. After putting his money in the fare box the guy just stands by the fare box looking at me. I look up from my task and I figured that he wanted me to say something so I look him in the face say, "Good Morning."

To which he responds, "Yea it is, now give me my change!" I glace down at the fare box and look at the digital read out and it shows an extra ninety-nine dollars on the meter. When Passengers put money into the fare box, Bus Drivers have to press the designated button that keeps track of the different categories of Passengers. There are nine buttons on the fare box, they are: adult fare; senior fare; student fare; adult monthly pass; senior monthly pass; student monthly pass; handicap adult monthly pass; handicap student monthly pass and miscellaneous. The Bus Driver presses the button that corresponds to the Passenger method of how he or she pays the fare. All bus passes are color coded, so the Bus Driver can tell at a glance the method of pay and if the bus pass is valid for that given month. The buttons on the fare box help Transit Systems keep track of rider-ship. Anyways, I look at the man and say, "Did you put a hundred dollar bill in there?"

The man replied, "Yea, now give me my change! I gotta go cause I'm late for work!"

I look at the man and said in the nicest and most professional way that I could, "Sir, Bus Drivers don't give change! I'll have to call my Dispatcher and see how he wants to handle this."

The man frantically exclaimed to me, "You got change in that bag there. I saw money when you were putting those papers back in there. Now please give me my change!" I don't know what that guy saw, but; there wasn't any money in that bag. All that was in that bag that he was talking about were new transfer packs, expired transfers and my designated transfer punch. I told the man that I would call my Dispatcher and see how they wanted to handle it. His response was, "Well do it now, cause I need to get goin to work!" I thought that his response was rather peculiar because I was driving the bus, not him. And besides, he was getting just a tad bit on my nerves with all of his little bossy demands.

I contacted Dispatch and after Dispatch answered, the conversation went something like this: Me, "I just had a Passenger put a hundred dollar bill in the fare box and he wants me to give him his change."

Dispatcher, "Did you tell the person that Bus Drivers don't give change."

Me, "Yes"

Dispatcher, "Well tell him to come over to the transit office about six tonight and I'll give him his change. That is the time that that bus will be out of service. I can't come out there now because I'm the only one here and besides I'd rather open the fare-box on transit property for security reasons. 10-4?"

I turned to the Passenger and relayed the message from my Dispatcher word for word so as not to have any misunderstanding. The Passengers reply was, "No way! I need my change now! I'm late for work as it is because of you."

My reply to him was, "Because of me? Sir, did you forget that you put the hundred dollar bill in the fare-box; not me."

The Passenger exclaimed," I want my change for my hundred and I want it now or I'm calling the cops!"

I said, "Let me get a hold of Dispatch; I'm sure we can work this out." It really didn't have anything to do with the Police; so why even get them involved. I picked up my radio and pressed the call button. When Dispatch responded I answered him in a very professional manner with, "The Passenger that put the hundred dollar bill in the fare-box wants his change immediately or he wants Police intervention. He is becoming very agitated. What do you want me to do?"

Dispatch replayed, "OK, we'll swap buses out. What is your status and what is your 20?"

I responded with, "I'm empty and I'm about five blocks from the transit office."

Dispatch, "OK, bring that bus back here right now and I'll have a bus parked out front for you. You do a quick pre-trip and I'll deal with the Passenger. 10-4?"

"OK, I'm on my way." Was my respond to Dispatch. I drove directly to the transit office and parked next to the bus that the Dispatcher had waiting out front for me. My Dispatcher came out of the building and introduced himself to the Passenger. They started arguing immediately. I watched as they both walked into the Transit office. I finished my pre-trip in a timely manner and was preparing to resume my route. Before I left the area, I went into the transit office to make sure that everything was under control. It was. I didn't think about that incident the rest of the day, I figured that it was over and done with.

At the end of the day I parked my bus at the transit garage and did a quick post trip. I had a few minutes before it was time to punch out so I decided to get a soda for the ride home. I opened my wallet and had a five dollar bill. I needed change. My first thought was to go see my Dispatcher because he had access to change. I walked over to the Dispatch office and my Dispatcher was sitting at his desk working. I said, "Excuse me Sir; but could I please get change for the soda machine?" He looked at me and started shaking his head and laughing. I instinctively said my famous one liner to him, "What?"

With a snicker on his face and a twinkle in his eye he answered back, "Man you sure know how to pick em!" Then I realized that he was referring to the guy that I had dropped off earlier who put the hundred in the fare-box. My Dispatcher was on a roll and continued talking, "Did you know that he intentionally put that hundred in there because he was too afraid to go to the bank across the street from were you picked him up on the bus. He was afraid because he thought that he had a bad check written and that the bank would keep his hundred dollar bill. Did you know that he also told me that he had no intention of riding the bus; he just wanted change! And further more, he told me that he works third shift and this was his day off? What do you think of that?"

I looked at the Dispatcher and said, "What can I say? Now could I please have my change so that I can get that soda?"

My Dispatcher continued talking as he was counting out my change, "There was a Driver doing a special assignment today for the library and she finished up just about the time that the hundred dollar bill guy was ready to leave so I asked her to stay a few more minutes and drop him off. Big surprise; she dropped him off at his car by the bus stop that you picked him up at. What do Yaw think of that?"

My Dispatcher laughed as he gave me change for the five.

I mockingly said, "So did you give that guy change for that hundred?"

With a smirk on his face that was more of a grin, my Dispatchers sarcastically said, "That guy learned two valuable lessons today."

I inquisitively responded with, "What were they?"

"Well, the first thing that he learned was that Bus Drivers don't ever give change, but: perhaps the main thing that he learned was; don't yell and scream at the Dispatcher and then expect him to give you change. Did I mention that I gave him his hundred dollar bill back? So in a nutshell, I guess you could say that Dispatchers don't give change either."

"Interesting", I exclaimed as I put my change from my five dollar bill in my wallet and was thoroughly enjoying my soda as I was exiting the transit office.

Chapter 18

Vacation Pictures

"Hey wanna see my vacation pictures?" That question is perhaps one of those questions that bring fear into the eyes of those being confronted with that dilemma. Terror, anger and a certain nauseous feeling are accompanied to those who must answer this inquiry. Individuals are brought to their knees and face that rock or a hard place decision when confronted with this social enigma. Nobody wants to or tries to hurt anybodies feelings, but; when that question is asked most individual's scruples are tested. It is not a matter of right or wrong; it is a matter of testing ones tolerance levels. Now really; who actually wants to look at home movies or pictures of somebody else's vacation? Most of the time, I don't like to especially if the pictures are of complete strangers. Do yaw know what I mean? Yes it is OK to look at one or two pictures, but; it never stops at one or two. It usually goes from one or two pictures into five to ten minutes. Most of us have all been confronted with that dilemma at one time or another in our lives.

One couple that rides the bus lives the alternate lifestyle.

It is their choice and they are happy with it, so; that is their business. This couple keeps to themselves and very few of the other bus Passengers even realize that this couple is happily married. There have been some; lets say awkward, moments that have come up on the bus, but; nobody was really offended and tempers were under control by all. I must say that this couple is perhaps two of the nicest people that I have ever met. They respect everybody else's life choices and wish other to respect theirs. This couple enjoys their privacy and do not publicly announce their lifestyle because of fear of reprisals by closed minded individuals. They will however tell selected individuals whom they feel will be comfortable with their situation. I happen to be one of those that they trust. I also have no problem with telling other people that this married couple are my friends. So with that being said and not wanting to offend or even give some sort of clue to their identity; I will not identify their gender in this story.

One morning the above mentioned married couple got on my bus. They had just returned from a well deserved vacation and were facing that "Back to reality check syndrome." They were talking about their vacation amongst themselves and I was sort of eavesdropping. Hey, what can I say? I'm seated three feet away and can hear their entire conversation. Not trying to pry or be noisy, I turned to them and said, "Hey, it sounds like you two enjoyed your vacation. Are those your vacation pictures?"

The one partner looked at me and said, "Do you want to see our vacation pictures?" Their partner that was seated next to them immediately interrupted before I could answer and said to their mate; "Are you sure that you want to show him our vacation pictures?" I could tell by the tone of their voice, that there was an emphasis on "our vacation pictures".

"Yea, why not? This will be fun!" Was the one partners reply.

"Well OK, but; don't laugh because we really had a good time," the apprehensive partner emphatically replied as their eyes met mine in the interior bus mirror.

I'm thinking to myself and wondering what I had gotten into. The one partner wants me to look at the vacation pictures because it will be fun, while: the other partner is showing anxiety and being somewhat concerned as to what I might see. Go for it I thought. And besides, I think that I can decide for myself if I like the pictures or not. I'm a big boy!

After a short discussion between themselves; they agreed that I could look at all the photographs. The one partner reached into a brown paper bag that they were carrying and produced a handful of pictures. The partner started sorting the pictures as if to put them in some kind of chronological order or something. By now I was at the end of the bus route and was in the process of parking the bus to take a short break. After the bus was parked and safely secured I turned in my seat to talk to the two lone Passengers on my bus. As I turned in the seat the one

Passenger was holding about three or four photographs out toward me so that I could look at them.

I took the pile of pictures and glanced down at the first picture on the stack. That picture was a picture of my two friends on vacation standing in front of a large sign. I could not read the writing on the sign because of the angle that the picture was taken. The two people in the picture looked happy and nothing was out of the ordinary, so; I took that picture and put it on the bottom of the stack of pictures and proceeded to looked at the second picture.

The second picture was in the same location, in front of the unreadable sign, as the first picture that was taken. The only exception was that instead of just two people, my friends, in the picture there was a crowd of people. I would say that there were at least twenty to twenty-five other people in the picture. The ages of the people in the second picture varied from I would say the mid-twenties to their late sixties. There was a get-together of young and old men and women. Again nothing looked out of the ordinary. I still hadn't a clue to who these people were. I looked up from the picture and looked at my two friends who were seated not more than three feet away. I was just about to ask them who these people were when the one partner said, "We met all those people at the camp." I figured that the picture was just a group shot of the outing and nothing more.

Looking up again I glanced at the second partner on the bus. They were looking at me and smiling. This was the partner who said, "It will be fun." The look on their face was one of those smirks that people usually have on their face when they're about to play a joke on someone else. I'm sure that you know the kind of smile that I'm talking about! I started to think that maybe I was falling into a practical joke or something, but; I didn't know. I continued to look at the second picture. After looking at the group photo for a second or two; I took the second picture and placed it on the bottom of the stack of pictures exposing to me the third picture.

As I was placing the picture on the bottom of the stack, I was thinking to myself, "Why am I looking at these pictures. You don't care. You're just trying to be nice. Hurry up and look at the pictures because you got a sandwich in your lunch box that you could be eating instead of looking at these stupid pictures, Mr. Nice guy." So I decide to hurry up.

As I started looking at the third picture I couldn't believe what I was looking at. I think that the picture that I was looking at was a picture of the same group of people that were in the second picture, but; the people in the second picture had clothes on and those people in the third picture were all nude. I'm talking standing around and posing in their birthday suits! The only stitch of clothing that I could see amongst the entire group of twenty-five or so men and women; was a hat that one of the elderly women was wearing. Please don't ask me to go into detail as to how I knew that she was elderly. I actually thought about gouging my eyes out like Socrates' Oedipus Rex did. I looked up from the picture that I'm sure that I was gawking at and sheepishly looked at my two so called friends. Who incidentally were laughing uncontrollably at me! I'm sure that was considered a Kodak moment for them, but; for me it was one of those uncomfortable moments that I wanted to be somewhere else and not there. Do yaw know what I mean?

I took the pile of pictures that I was now done looking at and held them out in front of me as to give them back. I had literally seen enough. This was one of those times where I actually got too much information. It seems with me it is either at one end of the spectrum or the other. The one partner reached out and took the pile of photographs that I was holding out in front of me and took them. As they were putting the pictures back into their brown paper bag they said, "We went to a Nudist Camp in Indiana for vacation."

"No, really! I never would have guessed that one let alone Indiana", was my sarcastic reply. After an awkward moment or two that seemed like eternity, I told my two friends that I was truly sorry for being nosy and interrupting their private conversation. They both sat there laughing uncontrollably at my expense. One of them exclaimed that the look on my face was priceless and they wished that they had taken a picture of my reactions. Guess I got what I deserved. Did I learn a lesson? Probably not!

I think that it literally took a couple days for the shock and embarrassment of that experience to wear off. Every time either one of those two individuals gets on my bus; I picture them nude. I really think that they can read my thoughts. They always smile at me and make little innuendo comments about that morning. I'm not sure if they're flirting with me or making fun of me. Whatever it is, I truly deserved it. To this day; that is why I don't ever ask to look at anybodies vacation pictures. I'm just trying to pass a little friendly advice on to you all and I hope that you all can learn from my foolishness.

Chapter 19

SKID MARKS!!

Some of the people that ride the bus, it would be fair to say, have problems with hygiene. I know that that might be hard to comprehend, but; it's true. Some of the stories that I tell are funny, but; to be honest, I also tell those stories that are repulsive. I was told by the Editor of one of our local newspapers that some things just shouldn't be said. I write about life on the Transit bus. I tell those stories because every thing is not perfect everyday and people are people. It's the truth, so get over it. Perhaps the general public aren't as naive as most of the newspaper editors think that we are. What a novel idea; it is called telling the truth! Maybe the newspapers should tell the truth more often and not sugar coat things because of fear of offending anyone.

Aside from the individuals who don't cover their mouth when they cough or sneeze; there is a group of individuals who use the Transit system that do things far worse than any antics that this group could come up with. The booger eating riders are hard to tolerate and literally make me nauseous, but: compared to this next story the booger eaters are sophisticated and refined. I'm talking about the group of bus riders who feel that body fluids and secretions are OK to share with their fellow riders. Yuck!!

Most of the Passengers that do ride the bus are regular riders on the bus. The Bus Driver usually know these individuals and are familiar with the Passengers little intricacies. For instance if a Passengers has an accident and unintentionally soils themselves while they're a Passenger on the bus; the Bus Driver, more often than not, won't forget a little incident like that. What happens in those cases is that the Bus Driver has to swap out buses and the bus that the Passenger had the mishap on

77

is taken out of service and gets a through cleaning. Little incidents like this take time away from the Driver and more than often causes the other Bus Passenger's inconvenient delays in getting to where they're going. All the paper work that is attached to these little problems is ridiculous, but; a formality that is in place for the public's best interest.

A young woman gets on my bus one day and nothing seemed out of the ordinary. This young woman was new to the area and she was trying to adjust to living in another city. The only thing that I really ever noticed out of the ordinary about this woman was her wardrobe. She always dressed comfortably by wearing tennis shoes, a light grey pair of jogging pants, a baseball cap and a dark sweatshirt. This is the only outfit that I have ever seen her wear. She dresses in this attire everyday. Weather doesn't affect her choice in clothing. If it's raining, snowing or the sun is shining one thing that is always constant is her being dressed in the same clothing. I remember that she first came on the scene in early fall and stayed in the area for about six months.

I can't really say if her wardrobe consisted of four articles of clothing or if she had a variety of sweatshirts and jogging pants. I don't know. Her baseball hat and tennis shoes were always clean and looked presentable.

Well anyways, she gets on the bus and after putting her coins in the fare box she sits down in the front seat to my right. I really try not to talk to the Passengers and hold conversations with them because of safety issues, but: most of the time the Passengers get to talking and it would be rude to just avoid them. A lot of times the Passengers talk to the Bus Driver because I think that they're lonely. My way of handling this dilemma is to pay attention to my driving and answer the Passenger's comments with a series of grunts and aha's. Ninety nine percent of the time that ploy works.

After driving about ten or twelve blocks and dropping Passengers off at the bus stops; the bus was empty except for the young woman who was seated to my right. After a few more blocks, the chime line sounded letting me know that the young woman wanted off at the next bus stop. She also verbally told me that she wanted off at the next stop when she was pulling the chime line. While doing this she stood up and acted like she was going to walk toward the front exit. I responded to her with, "Please remain seated until the bus comes to a complete stop." Of course she didn't listen and got up anyways. By the time I pulled up to the bus stop she was standing at the top of the exit stairs waiting to disembark the bus.

I stopped the bus at the bus stop and before I activated the lever that opens the front door; I always look toward the front doors to make sure that everything is safe before opening the doors. I do the same when closing the doors just to make sure that nothing will interfere with the doors operations. The Woman Passenger was standing at the top of the exit stairwell and was blocking my view from seeing the doors. She was standing about two feet from me and I had a really good view of her back and backside. As I glanced down her backside to see the door I could not help from looking at her backside. That is when I noticed a skid mark; please don't ask me to go into detail about it. Another thing that I also realized was that she was wearing her jogging pants inside out. The seam line and size tag was visible under the skid mark. I really couldn't believe what I was seeing. Not wanting to embarrass her or myself I immediately said to the young woman, "Excuse me, but; I think that you might have sat in something." I knew darn well that she didn't sit in something, but; that was the best I could do in a pinch.

The young woman immediately turned her head and looked over her left shoulder down behind her toward her buttocks. As she did that; she thrust her hips to the left so as she could see her backside. After slightly glancing at her backside she looked at me and without pausing said. "Oh, that's been like that for a few weeks now. I guess that I'm going to have to do a load of wash when I get home. And then she laughed as if it were a joke or something"

I snapped back at her and said, "You knew that that mess was back there and you still thought that it was OK to sit on a seat that other people sit on?"

"Yea, what's the difference? These buses are usually pig sties anyways." She snapped back at me.

I was mad and was going to get the last word in. Who in the world does she think that she is? As calmly as I could muster I said to her, "Two things. First, you are not welcome to get on any bus that I am driving with those filthy jogging pants on. Secondly, if I see you getting on any other bus with those filthy clothes on; I will talk to the other Driver and tell them about what happened today."

The young woman gave me a dirty look and said to me, "I'll never ride any bus that you drive again." And she stormed off the bus. As I was driving away thinking about what just had happened; she just stood there looking at me as I drove away.

A few days later down at the Transfer Center I saw the young woman whom I encountered that infamous day. She was still wearing the same color jogging pants and sweatshirt. I watched as she walked up to one of the buses and stood in line as if to board the bus. As she was standing in line she was pulling her sweatshirt down as if to cover her butt up. I was sure then that she didn't do the wash that night like she said that she was going to do. I immediately got off my bus and started to walk over to the bus that she was about to board. I wanted to talk to the other Driver and tell him about what had happened on my bus a few days earlier.

As I was walking toward the bus that the young woman was about to board; I watched as three other Bus Drivers walked up to her and started talking to her. I was to far away to hear what they were talking about, but; the discussion that she and the other Drivers were having was short and she made a hasty retreat out of the line. I walked up to the other Drivers and they were talking about skid marks. The one Driver turned to me and said, "Marty, if that lady that we were just talking to tries to get on your bus; call Dispatch and tell Dispatch that the lady with the skid marks is back,"

I said, "OK and started to walk back to my bus." I didn't like it and didn't think that is was right that some of the other Drivers were making little jokes and jabs about her issues. I guess that I felt bad for what I told her a couple days earlier. Perhaps if I had handled the situation differently, I could have helped her out rather than driven her to a so called exile. Some times I wonder why people do what they do, but; then again I keep forgetting that this is just a job and that we're not here to judge people. Nobody is perfect; I see examples of that everyday. Hey, all I have to do is look in the mirror to see a prime example of somebody that is not perfect.

Even though everything seemed fine on the outside with that young woman; there obviously are some issues that she is dealing with. Maybe she was homeless; I don't know. Whatever! I know that she knows right from wrong because when she was in line to get on that other bus; she was trying to pull her sweatshirt down to hide the skid marks that she had on her jogging pants.

I saw that young woman for a few weeks after that incident at the Transfer Center and then it was like she disappeared off the face of the earth. I have never had her as a Passenger on any of the buses I drove and as far as I can tell she never rode any of the city buses again. Perhaps if I had handled that situation differently the outcome would have been different. I think about what all the other Drivers had said so it wasn't just me who was caught up in her problems. It is times like that, that I gotta remember that I'm paid to drive the bus, not: judge my Passengers. More important; I need to remember that nobody is perfect.

Chapter 20

THE SNOW THROWER

I often wonder why people do things that are so profound that common sense is thrown out the window. I know for a fact, that I have done some pretty dumb things in my life. For instance, the time I held a piece of wood on my thigh and tried to drill a hole though the wood with an electric drill. Not to mention the time that I took a piece of pizza out of the hot oven and proceeded to take a huge bite out it. I try to forget little things like that, but; every time I look in the mirror and see the scars from the aftermath of those unthinkable moments, I realize how, let's say; how unintelligent, I really was at the moment. It seems that some individuals have moments like that everyday. I actually feel sorry for them, but; if they didn't do them, I'd have nothing to write about.

Along those same lines; one afternoon I'm sitting on the bus at the end of the line. This endpoint was at a high school and the other buses and I were assembled there waiting to resume our routes. We had about ten minutes to kill so all us Drivers were doing whatever. The weather was terrible in the morning and it had dropped about one foot of heavy wet snow. The roads were clear and in very good winter driving condition, but; the side-walks, on the other hand, were unshoveled and filled with snow. I was seated in a bus along with another Driver. We both were eating a sandwich that his wife had dropped off. It always seemed that when this Driver and I worked together, that either his wife or my wife were dropping food off for us. That's a good thing, but; most of the time our conversations revolved around exercise and our lack of participating in it. We always talk a good game about exercising, but; we seldom acted on it.

As we sat on the bus, we were talking about the weather; go figure. The weather forecast was calling for six to eight more inches of snow to fall and we both knew what that meant. Driving would turn treacherous. I trust my driving, but; I can't say that I trust the other Drivers on the road. Most of the people know how to drive in the snow because they're from this area and grew up driving in the snow. The best advice that I can give to anyone driving in the snow is to slow down. Most of the Drivers that have four wheel drive, think that just because they've got four wheel drive that they can go as fast as they want to. I don't care what yaw drive; when the roads are snowy and icy, you can't stop in a short distance.

Anyways, as we sat on the bus eating our lunch, we were watching a guy who was using a snow blower to clear the side walk. The guy wasn't really dressed properly to be blowing snow. I think that the light jacket, dress shoes and no gloves were a dead giveaway. I don't know who this guy was; all I know is that he was freezing his butt off.

The guy didn't know how to use the snow-blower either, which was a walk behind model. He was throwing the snow into the wind, which incidentally was blowing towards him. After a few minutes he looked like a walking snowman. The other Driver and I thought that it was kind of funny watching this guy. The other Driver made a comment about the snow-blower that the guy was using because the snow-blower's headlight kept going on and off. We both knew that we would be clearing off our sidewalks when we got off of work, but; for now it was fun watching someone else work. I guess it's a guy thing.

As we watched the guy blowing the snow, we started talking about snow-blower accidents. If you have ever used a snow-blower, you know that you never stick your hand down the chute to clear the snow. The chute is where the snow comes out of the snow-blower. At the bottom of the chute there is a blade that rotates very fast throwing the snow up into the chute and at the top of the chute there is a second blade that people forget about. This is where accidents happen. There is also a lever that the operator turns to blow the snow in the direction that the snow-blower operator wishes to throw the snow. Both of us were concerned about the fellow blowing the snow because he obviously never had used a snow blower before. We made up our minds that when the fellow blowing the snow got close to us, that we would mention some safety points to him. We didn't want him to get hurt.

As we sat there watching the guy he turned the snow-blower and started blowing the snow that was on the sidewalk in front of the buses. The headlight on the snow-blower kept going on and off. It was very noticeable and we both thought for sure that there was a short in the snow-blowers wiring. Being two guys that know everything that was our best conclusion as to why the headlight kept going on and off.

Both of us Drivers thought that clearing the snow from that area was a great idea because then the students could walk the path that he had cleared and maybe not get a lot of snow on the bus. It was a good thought on our part, but in reality; we both knew that the students would be playing in the snow, make snow angels and have snow fights before they get on the bus. Kids having fun, you know.

As we sat there on the bus we could hear the sound of the snow-blower coming up along side of the parked bus. As the guy blowing the snow walked the snow-blower along side of the bus we could hear the snow that was being expelled from the snow-blower as the snow hit the side of the bus. There was a thud thud at the rear side of the bus as the guy was blowing the snow against the side of the bus. We both looked into the right side mirror of the bus to get a good look at the guy working. The headlight on the snowblower was going on and off and the snow-blower was throwing snow.

The thuds got louder as the guy with the snow-blower walked the sidewalk along side of the bus. I said to my partner, "Don't yaw think that you should close the front door?"

"Why? When the guy gets to the front of the bus; he'll stop blowing the snow as he passes the front door. Give the guy a break will yaw!" the other Driver replied sarcastically.

As the thuds along side of the bus kept getting louder; I was becoming unsure if the guy blowing the snow would know what to do when he got to the front of the bus. I sat there with a ringside seat of what happened next. I was seated safely away from the door, while; the other Driver was seated in the Drivers seat facing the open bus door. As the snow-blower reached the front of the bus; the snow-blower's engine was blaring; the thuds on the bus were very loud and a mist of snow started to come into the front door of the bus. The thuds stopped and before the other Driver could react, masses of snow started to be blown into the open door of the bus. I sat there and watched as the snow-blower was blowing snow into the bus. The other Driver was getting plastered with the blown snow, but: I was safely tucked out of harms way.

Just as fast as the snow started coming into the bus door; it stopped abruptly. The thuds had stopped, but; the snow-blower engine was still running loudly. The guy that was blowing the snow started yelling frantically that he was sorry. The other Bus Driver was covered with snow. He kind of looked like Frosty the snowman to me!

The snow that was blown into the bus covered the side of the fare-box and was thrown around the Drivers area. Snow covered the dash board and there was a silhouette of the seated Bus Driver on the inside of the Drivers side window. My fellow Driver had a slight covering of snow on him. At first I thought that he was mad, but; then he started laughing. The guy that blew the snow into the bus was still being very apologetic. I just sat there in disbelief at what had just happened.

The guy got the snow-blower shut off and reached into the bus and started wiping the snow off of the floor with his bare hand. I asked my partner if he was OK. He just looked at me while he was shaking his head. He exclaimed," I should have closed the bleeping door!! You were right! Can Ya believe it?" I was more concerned if he was hurt, but; he was fine.

We now had a decision to make; should we call Dispatch or should we just clean the mess up. We didn't want to get the guy in trouble, but on the other hand; we had to make sure that nothing got wrecked. We chose to clean the mess up and see what we had. Besides, Dispatch would have told us to clean up the mess and get on with our routes, so; it would not be like we were doing anything wrong anyways.

The guy that blew the snow kept apologizing. He was truly sorry for what he had done. It took all three of us a couple minutes to get the mess cleaned up and except for some wet papers and pamphlets everything was fine. That is if you count a snow covered Bus-Driver as fine. The Driver, whom from hence on will be called Frosty, had a one piece coverall suit on and the snow came off with no problem. Was he lucky; if that snow blower had thrown a rock things would have been a lot different.

We asked the guy that was blowing the snow if he had ever blown snow before. No surprise that he said, "No." He said that the school custodian had given him a quick lesson on blowing snow and then disappeared. We asked the guy if he wanted us to show him anything on the snow-blower because we knew a little about them. We also mentioned to him that he needed to talk to the custodian about the short in the wiring system because the snow blower's headlight kept going on and off. That is when he said, "Yea, the electric chute doesn't work either."

I inquisitively asked, "What do you mean the electric chute doesn't work?"

The guy said, "I kept turning the toggle switch for the electric chute on and off and it never moved. When I would turn the snow-blower into the wind, the snow wouldn't go into the direction that I wanted it to go. That why I'm covered with snow. Hey man, when I was coming down the side of the bus; I was flicking that chute switch on and off and nothing happened"

Frosty said to the guy, "Could yaw show us that chute switch that you're talking about."

The guy said, "Sure", and pointed at the lone toggle switch on the snow-blowers handle.

Frosty and I looked at each other and said simultaneously, "That's the headlight switch."

The guy was looking at the snow-blower as if he were trying to figure something out. He then said, "Darn! I got the two mixed up. I thought that this lever down here was the light and that the chute was operated by that toggle switch." He then reached down and turned the lever and the chute turned as it was made to do. "Man do I feel dumb", he said.

Frosty and I tried not to laugh, but; we couldn't help but not to. We both kind of felt sorry for the guy, but; what could we say. We showed the guy how to properly use the snow-blower. We made sure that he knew not to put is hand into the chute. He understood what would happen. I had an extra pair of work gloves that I gave the guy. He said that his wife was on the way over to bring him some boots, gloves and winter clothing.

I asked the guy why he was blowing the snow dressed like that and he said that he was a new substitute teacher and wanted to make a good impression by helping out. Frosty was thawing out and I was flabbergasted. This guy was actually going to be teaching our youth. I thought to myself, I hope he is a better at giving instructions than following them.

The other buses started pulling out and we had to get going on our routes. The guy thanked us for showing him about the snow-blower and the safety tips. Before we left the guy apologized to Frosty at least a dozen more times. Frosty told him to forget about it and he resumed his route. I told the guy to be safe and started walking toward my bus. I abruptly turned back to the guy and said, "Hey I wouldn't mention anything to the custodian about any electrical malfunction on that snow-blower. It seems to be working just fine. See yaw later! Be safe!"

Chapter 21

PLEASE DON'T JUMP!

Every day on the bus is a new adventure. Bus Drivers see things from a view that others don't. We see what people are doing in their vehicles when we're driving down the road or when we are parked beside them at the stop and go lights. If most of these parents knew the habits of their teenage Drivers: they would be mortified and not let these Kids drive. These Parents think that the stories that they see on the evening 6 O'clock news could never be their Kids, but; their sadly mistaken. The Kids talk on the phone, text message, play with the radio and mess around with the other Passengers. If a boy and girl are sitting along side one and other they could be mistaken for a Siamese Twins. I mean give me a break. They sit there with their leg entangled; their arms all over the other person and sometimes you can't tell whose head belongs to whose body.

The way that the teenaged girls sit in the Drivers seat is surreal. I mean they look as if their sitting on the couch or a big comfy chair. Quite a few of them drive with their left knee even with their head. If they need to react fast they couldn't. The teenage boys when they're driving, it's like they're lying down. When you look at them through the front windshield of the car that they're driving; all you can see are the front view of half of their heads. No really, if you didn't know that they were driving reclined you would think that most teenaged boys that were driving were less than four feet tall when they stood up.

Whatever all these teenaged Drivers learned in Drivers education class; was left in Drivers education class. I'm not saying that all teenagers have bad driving habits. I'm saying the ones that do have bad habits were taught these habits from their peers and adults. Heck, I bet you in

Drivers education class they were taught to try to stop when you see the upcoming signal turn from green to yellow. Not go like a bat out of heck just to make the light before it turns red. Any Driver that does not check the intersection before they enter it is an accident waiting to happen.

Like I said, we Bus Drivers see to many things. Traffic accidents; utility break downs; water main breaks; fights and whatever. A lot of times we get Passengers on the buses who are trying to make it on their own. These individuals are challenged with obstacles that are either physical or mental. I applaud these individuals for their efforts. These individuals always have someone looking over their shoulders and trying to help them succeed. I've had transition and case workers come on my bus and start asking me questions about certain riders. I usually don't know nothing when people start asking me questions about bus Passengers, but; if I feel that the person asking the questions are trying to help the person, it's a different story. Before these team members start asking any questions they usually produce more identification then any normal person would actually think of carrying on their person. This is what I would prefer that someone in that position would do.

The one Passenger that they were inquiring about to me one day is a regular rider. I have never had any problems with him and he is very friendly to the other Passengers. The only thing that I really noticed different about this fellow was that he needed to change his clothes more often. He wears the same clothes if its winter or summer, with that being a sweatshirt and jogging pants. This fellow needs to be wearing a belt or a piece of rope to hold his drawers up, too; because he is constantly pulling his jogging pants up after they get past his lower belly.

The sweatshirt, that he wears, is stained in front with leftovers from past meals that he has eaten. Or should I say has tried to eat and missed his mouth. The team members were telling me that this fellow lives in a group home and is being evaluated to have his own living quarters. They said that they couldn't give me a lot of pertinent information because of privacy laws, but; if I could answer some general questions about him it would be a big help to them in helping him out. That is why I agreed to answer the questions about him. I answered about ten general questions about him to the transition team. Since the team members were asking me questions, I felt that it would be fair for me to ask them a question or two.

My question was, "Why do the people in charge allow this man to leave the group home dressed like he does? I mean give the guy a break! He wears the same clothes everyday of the year. He's got a mess on his sweatshirt that obviously has been there for a while and for heaven sake, gives the man a belt to hold his pants up." The team members both looked at me as if they knew exactly what I was talking about.

The one team member sheepishly said, "I'm the person in charge of the group home and we have been working on those problems for a long time. He actually has a nice wardrobe at the group home, but; the only clothes that he ever wears are those big jogging pants and that sweatshirt. And yes, I agree whole heartedly that he need to wear a belt, but; he won't wear one because there are no belt loops in the jogging pants. He has made a lot of progress the past couple of months about getting his clothes washed. I'm sure getting him to wear a belt in the near future is a possible probability."

I was starting to feel as if I were a member on their transition team. Heck, I just want to help the guy, that's all. I just read too much into the things that I see. Well I'm not on the transition team because I am a Bus Driver. And that is what I should be doing now because this conversation was putting me behind schedule. So, I told the two transition team members, "Thank you for asking me about that fellow, but: I have a schedule to keep and I have to get going. If you have anymore questions, please contact the transit office. I'm sure that they can help you help him. Got to go! Have a nice day." The transition members got off of my bus and I resumed my route. I felt that I did my part to help this guy out. After all everybody deserves a break now and then.

I saw the fellow that they had asked me about, regularly on the bus after that conversation. I never mention anything about that conversation to him. If he would have asked me about it, I would have told him everything. I would not have lied to him. Yea there was a dramatic change in his clothes. He was still wearing a sweatshirt and baggy jogging pants, but; they were clean. I was astounded at the change. I also noticed that he had gotten his hair cut and was wearing a new pair of designer tennis shoes. It was a noticeable change for him. I would say that he was headed in the right direction. He also seemed to talk more and be more open, but; he still had some childish tendencies to over come.

One day as he was getting off of the bus at the front stairwell, he turned to me and said, "Hey Marty, watch this." I could tell that he was going to jump off of the second step onto the curb.

I said to him, "Don't jump, you could hurt yourself. And beside you'll get your new shoes dirty!" Too late! He jumped off of the bus and onto the curb. He landed with his feet spread about shoulder width apart and both of his feet hit the ground at the same time. Like I've been saying, we Bus Drivers see everything. He landed firmly on the ground with his feet planted. If I were an Olympic Judge I'd probably have give him a seven for his landing. Well I am not an Olympic Judge; I'm a Bus Driver. This is what happened next. When he landed, he and I both got a surprise. His belt less jogging pants fell to his ankles. He stood there as if he were surprised and didn't know what to do next.

I said to him, "Pull your pants up before somebody see's ya!" Although at the time it seemed like the right thing to tell him to do, I didn't know what I was in for. You see, he was standing outside of the bus door facing away from me. I was seated in the Bus Drivers seat and looking down at him. His jogging pants were on the ground at his ankles and his sweatshirt was hanging down covering his backside. As he dropped his arms straight down toward his shoes and bent over forward at the waist; that's when I realized that he wasn't wearing any underwear. I mean it happen so fast that I didn't have time to look away.

There he stood bent over mooning me. My immediate thought was to gouge my eye's out, but; that wasn't an option because I didn't have anything in my hands to do it with. I thought about using my fingers, but; realize that I needed my eyes to drive the bus. I just sat there gawking. I thought to myself; I don't need to see things like that. I'm talking about a full moon. I wanted to gag. If there had been a werewolf on the bus or in the near vicinity, I'm sure that they would have started howling. I was lucky; there was no one else on the bus. As I turned away from looking at his bare behind and the vast acreage of unknown territory I yelled to him, "Pull your pants up before somebody see's ya!" I then thought to myself, those were the same words that got you in this position in the first place, keep your mouth shut!

My eyes were burning as I scoped the surrounding area hoping that nobody was around to witness the sight. I was afraid that some kid would be waiting for the bus and see something that they shouldn't be a seeing. It just so happens at that bus stop, there is a park bench located directly even where the buses stop. Again my luck held out. I parked the bus even with the park bench like I was instructed to do by my superiors. This park bench is usually occupied by the senior women that live in the nearby apartment complex. I'm sure that the sight of this nude man would have caused them all sorts of issues if they had been sitting on the park bench enjoying the day.

The guy got his pants pulled up and stood there for a second or two. He then turned toward me and said," I'm sorry Marty."

My eyes were just getting back to normal focus and I was trying to get that thought of what I saw out of my mind. I scolded him with my response, "You should be! Did you know that in some countries that something like that could make us legally married?" I could tell that he was embarrassed and was sorry. I said to him, "Now you see why everybody wants you to wear a stupid belt."

He sheepishly replied, "I'll always wear a belt now. Do ya think that I should start wearing underwear too?"

My mind was just about ready to over flow from to much information when I regained my senses. I said to him, "Normal people do wear underwear all the time. What do you think?" He looked at me and gave me a nod that he understood. He said, "See ya later Marty!"

I'm thinking that I'd seen too much already. I said to myself drop it. You got your point across now forget about it. As he walked away I said to him," You think about what happened to day and have a nice day, OK?" He walked away from the bus stop and didn't look back. He did however raise his right arm and hand up to acknowledge the comment I had made to him.

I continued my route and thought about the ordeal the remainder of the day. At the end of the day, I went home and told my wife about what had happened. A lot of help she was. She just shook her head and laughed. I asked her if she thought that if I washed my eyes out with hot water or maybe used ice packs on them that the pain would go away. She just went about her business. I kept telling myself that I could make it through anything after that tribulation. I also convinced myself that perhaps that wasn't the worst thing that I have ever seen. Pretty close to number one, but; still a long way from the worst. As for the fellow that wears the jogging pants and sweatshirt. He still does, but; his ensemble now includes a belt. Amen!!

Chapter 22

THE ROLE MODEL

Everybody looks up to someone. When you're a kid, it seems that your choices are usually limited. We would hope that our young adults choose role models that are productive and viable assets to society, but; many times their choices are limited. Ya, they could choose an athletic superstar for a role model and then be disappointed by his or her negative behaviors. After something like that happens the kid starts second guessing themselves. And beside they never get a chance to actually know or meet their chosen role model so in time they realize that they made a poor choice. They won't admit it to you so don't even ask them. I don't think that Kids realize how important it is to try to find a person whom they want to be like. I think the way that it supposed to work is that role models should be from individuals who the kid knows. Maybe these role models should come from at home. Gee, what a novel idea. Maybe if mom or dad would talk to the Kids more often, the Kids could make better choices.

I know that many of the Kids that do ride the buses don't have a dad at home. Maybe a brother in-law or an uncle should step up to the plate, but then again; that too would take an effort. If these Kids were told of the hardships that a single parent faces, maybe their choices wouldn't be so hard. Sometimes Kids for whatever reason will pick another kid to try to copy their behaviors. This chosen role model lasts until such time when the chosen role model disappoints or fails to meet the choosers' expectations.

I recall this one young adult who was quite a bit larger in size than the Kids that he hung around with. These Kids were in middle school and were very susceptible to peer pressure. I think that the big kid was a kind of a security blanket for all the Kids that hung around him. When he got on the bus; Kids would actually push and shove one another just to sit by this big kid. There were never any fights, but; at times it came real close. If the big kid would say something all those that were sitting by him emphatically agreed to anything that he said. Anything he would do all the Kids seated near him would copy. If he sat on the seat and crossed his legs; all the other Kids would cross their legs in the same manner as his. In a way it was kind of comical watching how things were playing out. I observed many instances, through my interior bus mirror, where anything that this kid did was copied by his peers. At times, I think the big kid just wanted to be left alone and didn't really know how to go about telling the other Kids his wishes. If he was enjoying all the attention, he really never showed it.

Kid will be Kids and as time would have it, one day on the bus the big kid spoke the "N" word in a conversation that he was having with one of his worshipers. I immediately spoke up and said to the young man, "Excuse me, but: we don't use the "N" word on my bus! So in the future, I would very much appreciate it that you do not use it. If you feel that you must use that word; I would prefer it if you rode another bus. Do you understand me?"

When the Kids are on my bus, they know what I expect out of them. I do not allow horseplay or foul language. My definition of horseplay is any activity where there is a chance of someone getting hurt. Foul language includes any swear words or any word that makes fun of or is demeaning to any ethnic or religious group. The "N" word is strictly prohibited and under no circumstances can it be used on my bus in any context. Many times young adults will refer to themselves as the "N" word and say that it is OK because the word is in the dictionary. I really don't care if it's in the dictionary or not; don't use it on my bus! I've had numerous conversations with many young adults of various ethnic backgrounds about using that word. If there is going to be trouble on the bus, that word is usually the catalyst. I've spoken with many a young adult and stressed to them that that racial slur in particular not only degrades an ethnic group, but; also degrades and labels the user of the word as well.

The big kid that had said the "N" word looked at me in the interior mirror. The look on his face was that of one knowing that he had done something wrong. He sat looking at me as if he were thinking of what he could say to retaliate to my comment. The Kids that were sitting around the big kid started making little comments directed toward me. They were protecting him. I think that they were trying to get me to get mad at them and lose my temper. That surely wasn't going to happen because I know that if that would happen; I would lose control of the situation and we would just get in a yelling contest that nobody would win. So I just sat there as I was being verbally assaulted. Some of the comments were, "It's a free country; we can say what we want." And "Mind your own business; we're having a private conversation." I didn't respond I just kept driving the bus.

I knew that I had to defuse the situation. Some of the Kids, those that were seated by the big kid, kept making demeaning comments directed at me. Someone pulled the chime line indicating that they wanted off at the next stop, so; I figured that it was time to defuse the situation. When I pulled over to the curb I opened the front and rear doors of the bus; about four or five students got off the bus when I opened the doors at the bus stop. This was their normal bus stop and it was nothing out of the ordinary. The group of Kids that were sitting around the big kid stopped their verbal assault and they were waiting to see what the big kid was going to do or say. I just sat there in the Drivers seat waiting for the disembarking Passengers to clear the doors. I continued looking into the interior mirror watching the coach of the bus and the big kid happened to be in my line of sight. The big kid leaned forward in his seat and said in a rather loud voice, "Excuse me sir" and paused. The other Kids just sat there waiting and listening to what he was going to do or say.

Much to my surprise, the big kid courteously said in a very apologetic manner, "Please accept my sincere apology for using that word. I'm sorry and I will try my best to never say it again."

My response was, "Apology accepted and thank you for understanding." I was getting ready to resume with my route. Quite a few of the Kids couldn't believe what had just happened. Some just sat there while some of the others talked amongst themselves. The big kid sat there looking out of the window. I think that he was a little embarrassed at the whole incident. One of the smaller Kids started making idle threats directed at me. He then said the "N" word. Before I could even respond the big kid interjected. He said very sternly to the smaller kid, "Knock it off! The Bus Driver is right."

The smaller kid who had used the "N" word said, "What do you mean he's right?"

The big kid responded with, "Hey, next year we go to High school. Don't you think we should start acting our age? You know if we use that word in high school; I'm sure that we would get into big trouble."

"I can use any words that I want to use," the smaller kid replied. He then got up from the seat and walked toward the front exit of the bus. I watched in the mirror as he made his way forward. I wasn't sure how he was going to react when he got up by me so I unfasten my seat belt. I did it in a way as to not make it noticeable to him. When he got to the front stairwell he turned his head and looked at me. He just shook his head and got off the bus. I close the doors, fasten my seat belt and resumed my route.

The big kid and those that remained on the bus started talking between themselves. I couldn't hear the conversation, but; whatever they were talking about the smaller Kids were listening to the big kid. I drove on. One by one I dropped off the Kids at their desired stops. Like I always do; I watched each and every one of them in my interior mirror. Not one of them even realized that I was watching them. When I got to the stop of the big kid, he got up from the seat and looked directly at me in the mirror. As my eyes met his in the mirror; he gave me thumbs up. He then turned and got off the bus.

That big kid and those that worship him still ride the bus. The one smaller kid that had the argument with the big kid still sits with and emulated all the things that the big kid does. I guess he still has the big kid as a role model. Since that day I've noticed a change in that group of Kids. They all act a little bit more grownup. Of course they're still Kids and many times their conversations get a little loud. All I can say is that I have never had any more problems with that group of young adults concerning their language or choice of words. I guess that big kid turned out to be a pretty good role model after all. It's too bad that some of the immature adults that ride my bus weren't on the bus that day to see how things can change by cleaning up their vocabularies.

Chapter 23

HE WON'T CALL THE COPS

I see things on the bus that just make me laugh. Everybody is the same regardless of their ethnic background or gender. I think that many students that ride the bus try to put on an image that they're tougher than they really are. In a way this is good, but; it also makes individuals very vulnerable when something happens to challenge that image. It's OK to have a high self esteem and greater than thou attitude, but; there is also a time to curb your enthusiasm and cockiness as well.

Some individuals want to give the personification that they are tougher than anybody else and want everybody in the immediate area to recognize them as such. They think that all the rules on the bus apply to everyone else and not them. Not on my bus. I treat everybody the same and expect all my riders to follow the rules. Those that do ride my bus know what I expect out of them and had better follow the rules if they want to continue riding the bus. We Bus Drivers have numerous resources available to us to handle most situations. At any time I can pick up my radio and contact Dispatch for help. I noticed that most of the time when riders are verbally confronted, in a professional manner, about their behavior they conform to the rules.

One afternoon a group of young adults got on the bus that I was driving. I picked this group up at a local high school. It was obvious to me that this group of students had just been to a pep rally. It was September and a Friday; so, that meant a big football game was on tap for later in the day. The group was a little rowdy and they were showing their team spirit by wearing team colors and carrying banners. It was just high school Kids having a good time. I though it to be neat and told them that I hoped that their team win tonight. Lot of high fives and trash talk about the other team was going on. Nobody was out of control, everybody was just having fun.

I continued my route and kept a good eye on my group of High School students as I drove on. I knew that they would be getting off the bus in a short time, so; as long as they kept their enthusiasm in somewhat of a civil manner, I could handle them. I drove on. I glanced in my interior mirror scanning the coach when something to my right caught my eye. A student seated not more than three feet away from me started playing with a cigarette lighter. I turned to him and said," You need to put that lighter away now and stop playing with it!"

When I said that to him I challenged him in front of his peers and he didn't like it. He sarcastically retorted back, "What are you gonna do? You gonna call the Police on me?"

I said to him in a calm voice, "If you don't stop; I have no problem with calling the Police. So I'm saying one last time; put it away now!"

"You won't call the cops!!" He replied and he lite the lighter again. This was one of those Kids who wanted to be the center of attention and he definitely had my attention. I remember this young adult from a previous incident where he was eating potato chips on the bus and I told him in front of his peers that there was no eating on the bus. What he did was, rather than put the chips away; He got off the bus and made the comment to me, "You can't tell me what to do!" He did this because he wanted to show off in front of his peers. It seemed then that he had this image that he had to uphold. Him getting off the bus didn't bother me one way or another. All I cared about was that he stopped eating the chips on the bus. I don't yell at the Kids on the bus because I try to be smarter than them. Beside, nobody ever wins those types of arguments.

It was time for a reality check!! I drive the bus and I don't get paid to argue. I knew that and now he was going to realize it. Safety first on my bus! I picked up my radio and asked Dispatch for assistance. At that time I informed Dispatch of my location and my Passenger status. The young adult was watching me the entire time that I was speaking with Dispatch. He must have thought that I was joking because he lit the lighter again and muttered something under his breathe to the Kids that were sitting with him. Big joke I thought to myself. Hey, an open flame and a bus full of people? Not on my Bus! I told Dispatch what the young man was doing and asked how I should handle the situation. Dispatch said," We're not going to deal with it! I'm contacting the Police. Secure your bus and wait for the Police to arrive. 10-4?"

My response was, "10-4." I have an open radio and the young adult heard the entire conversation that I had with my Dispatcher. A few of the Kids that were sitting by him got up and moved a few seats back from where he was sitting. These Kids knew me and I guess that they wanted a front row seat when the Police arrived. That left the kid playing with the lighter and four of his friends. They were all making little comments. The lighter flicker kept saying, "He won't call the cops!! He's just bluffing!!"

I just sat in the Drivers seat listening, watching and waiting. Hey, I'm good at waiting. Man, I could do that all day. What more could I ask for. First I'm getting paid for not doing anything and secondly I know that I'm going to have company, the Police, in a minute or two. I didn't respond to any of the comments being thrown at me because I didn't want the situation to get entirely out of hand.

About two minutes went by and the first of two Police squad cars arrived. There was no fan fare in the form of sirens or lights, but; the Police car presence was more than enough to get a reaction from the lighter flicker and his friends. Two of the Kids that were sitting by the lighter flicker got up and walked to the open rear door of the bus and made a quick retreat away from the bus. The two remaining Kids got up and went and sat down on the rear seat of the bus by another group of Kids. That left the kid that was flicking the lighter seated by himself. I turned and looked at the kid. The look on his face was that of disbelief. He looked at the squad car that was parked in front of the bus and then looked me straight in the face. He said in a rather shaky voice, "you called the Police on me. I was just kidding around; I didn't want to hurt anyone."

About that time the Police officer started getting out of the Police squad that was parked in front of the bus. At the rear of the bus another squad car pulled up. A burly Police officer walked from that squad to the rear door of the bus blocking the door making it impossible for anybody to get out of that door. The lighter flicker just watched what was going on around him. Then without pause the lighter flicker started to cry and whimper like a baby.

I just sat there looking at him. I guess that he wasn't as tough as he appeared to be. He took the lighter that he had in his hand and put it in his front pant pocket. He looked at me and whimpered, "Am I going to go to jail? I'm sorry!"

I responded with, "I don't know. You got to deal with these guys now. It's out of my hands." About that time a Police officer walked through the front entrance of the bus and said to me, "Is there a problem here?"

I said, "Yes officer, this young adult, I pointed my finger toward the lighter flicker, has a cigarette lighter and was playing with it. I told him numerous times to put it away and he didn't. I have to worry about all my Passengers, besides; there are federal laws concerning open flames on a bus. I just want him off the bus. Maybe if he walked for a while; he could think about his actions."

The Police officer gave a stern look at the whimpering young man seated in front of him and said,' Do you have a cigarette lighter on your person?" Without hesitation the young man produced the cigarette lighter. The Police officer reached out and took the lighter from the frightened Passenger. "If you had tried to lie or was hesitant about producing the lighter; you probably would have had a free ride to the Police station," the officer hardheartedly told the young man. "Now get up and get off the bus so that we can talk to you," Said the officer. The ten or so remaining students heard the entire conversation.

The frightened, crying young adult stood up and started to walk off the bus with the Police officer. As he was leaving the bus, the red faced young man turned toward me and said, "I'm sorry for any trouble that I might have caused. You will never have any problems with me again when I ride the bus." The Police officer then escorted the young man off the bus toward the parked Police car. The officer that was at the rear door watched as the officer at the front door placed the young man in the Police car. He then looked at the remaining students on the bus and said, "Any of you guys got any cigarette lighters?" With that being said at least eight of the ten remaining students, without pausing or hesitating, produced cigarette lighters. The burly officer held his hand out and each one of the Kids got up from their seats and gave their cigarette lighter to the officer. The officer seemed kind of surprised at the reaction that he had gotten from the group.

The burly officer then said, "OK, How many of you guys got tobacco products on you?" With that being said, at least seven of the ten Kids produced cigarettes and one kid had a tin of chewing tobacco. I'm watching the entire show through my interior mirror. The big burly officer had his hands full of confiscated items now. From my Bus Drivers seat I said, "Excuse me officer, would you like a bag for all that stuff?"

He responded with, 'Ya, You got one?" I reached into my carryon bag and I held up a plastic garbage bag that I always keep handy. The gigantic officer walked up to me and put the items in the plastic bag that I held open for him. I looked at the officer and we both were almost laughing. I said to the Police officer, "Now might be a good time to ask if they know where Jimmy Hoffa is. You know what I mean?" He rolled his eyes and walked back to the rear of the bus.

"You guys wait here! I'll be right back," the officer told the now frighten group of Kids. He went to the squad car and had a brief conversation with the other officer. After about five minutes both of the officers came to the front door of the bus and the large burly officer said, "We're going to take this group of Kids off your bus. My partner and I are going to try to figure out what we can do or say to maybe straighten this group out." After saying that; the two officers went to the rear of the bus and escorted the entire group of young adults off of the bus. I was the only one left on the bus and that was fine with me.

I called Dispatch and told them what had happened. Dispatch told me to make sure that I wrote an incident report just in case something comes of this. I then continued with my route. About an hour later, I drove past the location where the incident had happened. All the Kids were gone, but; the two squad cars were parked there. I didn't stop to see what the outcome was; I just waved to the officers as I drove by. The next day was Saturday and I was driving the same route that I had the day before. A student got on my bus and said that she was one of the students that had been taken off my bus the night before by the Police. She told me that the two Police officers called each of the student's parents and informed them of what had happened on the bus. She said the one boy that was playing with the cigarette lighter got a ticket for disorderly conduct. She told me that she was sorry and had learned her lesson. I accepted her apology.

That Monday, the boy that had gotten the disorderly conduct ticket got on my bus. Before he got on the bus he asked me if it would be OK with me if he rode on the bus. He said that he had learned a lesson and I would never have a problem with him again. I said to him, "I have no problem with you riding the bus as long as you behave yourself." He replied with a nodding of his head and took a seat about midway down the aisle of the coach. I always scan the interior mirror of my bus just to keep an eye of what is going on inside the bus. There were at least fifteen to twenty students on the bus. I recognized many of them as being on the bus the Friday before. Every one of them was being very cordial and pretty much keeping to themselves.

I never mentioned anything to any of those Kids again about that Friday night incident. I do know this; each and every one of those young adults learned that honesty is the best policy. The look in each and every one of those kid's eyes showed me that they knew that that burly Police officer meant business. And if anyone of them would have tried to lie, they would have gotten that free ride to the Police station. I also have never seen any of those Kids with any kind of smoking paraphernalia. What ever those two Police officers told those Kids. It sunk in and in this case it worked.

It took a few weeks for the young adults to forgive the kid that was playing with the lighter. After all, if he had put his lighter away and not have tried to be a wise guy; all the other Kids wouldn't have gotten in trouble. I think that it's funny how things all work out for the best.

Chapter 24

THE FIELD TRIP

Kids love riding the buses and streetcars in our community. Our community has a vintage streetcar collection that travels on a two mile rail loop. A lot of the taxpayers in our community call it the "Trolley to nowhere." Some transit officials call it their "Little Toy Train" and treat the streetcars as such. The city Bus Drivers operates the streetcars and the buses. The streetcars charges twenty-five cents per ride per person. Children under five years of age ride for free. Passengers can also use their monthly bus pass to ride the streetcar. The Transit Department does accept groups and for a fixed rate will rent one of the streetcars out for weddings, parties and social events. Even thought the cost is minimal; many individuals complain about the price of riding or renting the streetcar.

The streetcar ridership total is perhaps 60,000 per year and most of the operating costs for the streetcars are in the transits departments' budget. Maintenance of the streetcars is a major drawback because of their age, but; overall it's all right. The streetcar may bring in approximately fifteen thousand dollars a year in revenue. That doesn't even come close to covering the expenses of a streetcar motorman; multiply mechanics; operating cost and general maintenance costs. Overall the streetcar is good for our community because of the people that come to our community to visit the streetcar. The greatest benefactors are the area merchants.

Kids love the streetcar. I think it is the ambient sounds that the streetcars make. I myself love to hear the clickity clack of the wheels on the rail. It's very nostalgic. Some individuals who think that they know everything about everything always correct the Kids and tell the Kids that it is a trolley; not a streetcar. Who cares? Some people think that they need to put their two cents in everybody else's business. Just leave the Kids alone.

One morning while I was operating the streetcar, I was informed by Dispatch that I would be having three groups of students on their year end school trip. The Passengers would be first and second grader students, Teachers and Chaperones. The groups would be divided into groups of thirty. I was kind of excited because all the Kids would be laughing and smiling. I know quite a few of the Kids because they ride the streetcar regularly. It would be a fun day for all.

I picked the first group of thirty up and our destination was the new museum. The new museum is located about ten blocks from the Transfer Center where I was picking up the groups. The ride to the new museum is just a little under the half way point of the streetcar ride. The streetcar ride started with all the Kids singing a song. The song that they were singing was the one school bus song modified to include the streetcars. You know the song: The wheels on the streetcar go round and round; round and round; round and round. I know that you'll have that song in your head the rest of the day; Sorry!

About three block into the ride, at one of the streetcar scheduled stops, there was a man waiting to ride the streetcar. He was seated on the bench that was located at the streetcar stop. I recognized the man as a resident who lives in the immediate area. I also knew that this individual had a problem with limiting his consumption of alcoholic beverages. To not sugar coat it; the guy had a bad drinking problem. I know this to be true because I've dealt with him many times when he was in an inebriated state. All the Passengers on the streetcar were singing and having a good time and I had to make a decision of what to do.

I pulled the streetcar up to the stop and I immediately noticed that the guy had filthy clothes on and a substance, what appeared to be vomit, on the front of his shirt. I instantaneously made up my mind that I didn't want this fellow on the streetcar. I didn't think that a six or seven year older should remember their year-end field trip with memories of celebrating it with a guy with vomit on his shirt and the accompanying smell of alcohol and cigarettes. I opened the streetcar doors and said to the fellow that the streetcar was full and that he could probably walk to wherever he was going faster.

He looked at me and said in a rather disappointed voice, "I'll get the next one." I knew that meant me as the next one because I had the only streetcar out on the tracks that day.

I replied to him, "Chances are that one will be filled too, because we have school tours today. I've got three trips to the new museum with the tours, so just wait here if you want. If you're in a big hurry you could probably walk there faster. I'll check you out on my next round OK?"

He said, "I'll wait."

I checked my mirrors and made sure it was safe to go; then I accelerated the streetcar and headed down the tracks toward the new museum. A couple teachers, which were seated near the front of the streetcar, witnessed the conversation that I had with the guy on the bench and they said to me in a concerned manner, "Are we going to have to put up with him all morning?"

I responded with, "He does have the right to ride the streetcar. To be fair to him; I'm not going to pick up any other Passengers on the route while this tour is going on." I contacted Dispatch and told them what was happening. Their response was to do the best that I can. The good thing about it was that it was an off peak time and I just had three runs to make to get all the Kids to the new museum. I was on the first run so that meant just two left. The bad news was the only way to get to the new museum was to pass the guy sitting on the bench.

I dropped the first group off at the new museum and proceeded back to the Transit Center to pick up the second group. As I pulled the streetcar up to the Transit Center everybody at the stop was singing and having a good time. I motioned with my hand to a teacher to move the group of Kids back away from the streetcar rails a little further. They were already away from the tracks, but; why take a chance of something happening. I pulled the streetcar in front of the Transit Center and opened the front doors of the streetcar.   A Teacher came on board and with the help of a Chaperon: seated thirty ecstatic children on the streetcar. In a short time, group two was on their way to the new museum. I love to hear the sound of children laughing and having a good time. It makes me reminisce of my grandchildren and my childhood.

I drove the streetcar along and was hoping that the fellow that was sitting on the bench wouldn't be there, but; there he was. I didn't want to make the fellow think that I was avoiding him, so; I stopped the streetcar in front of the bench that he was seated on and opened the streetcar doors. I said to the guy. "Remember, I got this group and one more, then I'll pick yaw up OK?"

"I'll wait," he muttered back.

"Good," I said to myself. I closed the streetcar doors and continued on to the new museum. One of the teachers made a comment about the individual that was seated on the bench. I didn't say anything I just sat there and drove the streetcar. The comments that the teacher was making about the man weren't bad, but; I felt that the conversation should be focused on the Kids and not on his predicament. There are two museums in our city; the new one and the old one. We were headed to the new museum, but; the streetcar rails pasted the old museum as well. As the streetcar approached the old museum, I made a comment to the group on the streetcar that a dinosaur exhibit was going to be placed permanently in the building. I really wanted the teacher to change their topic. It worked. The teacher that was making the comments about the man on the bench started talking about dinosaurs to the children on the streetcar. Before we knew it we were at the new museum. Group two was disembarking in an orderly fashion and I would soon be on my way for the final group.

I left the new museum and was headed back toward the Transfer Center. I got to the Transfer Center and the third group was waiting. This group seemed to be more excited than the first two groups. As I pulled the streetcar up to the stop I could see the electricity in the air that the group was generating. This was going to be a fun ride. The group of thirty boarded the streetcar and we were soon on our way. Like the other groups before; this group was singing too.

As I motored toward the new museum, I approached the bench where the man was sitting on the bench waiting for me and an empty streetcar. As I drove past the man I waved to him. To my surprise he waved back. I thought to myself, "This guy really has patients." I find it amusing how people act differently to situations. This guy really wanted to ride the streetcar or he was just too lazy to walk. It didn't matter to me because I felt that I did the Kids justice by not letting him on the streetcar. The one consolation to me was that he seemed to accept the situation. Whatever! I continued toward the new museum.

This group on the streetcar was extremely loud and having a good time. I think that it's neat the way children can make adults laugh with their laughter. You know what I mean? The time flew by and before I knew it; we were at the new museum. I pulled the streetcar up to the new museum and opened the front doors of the streetcar. As the first Passenger, a teacher, walked past me; they gave me a high five and said, "Thanks, we'll see yaw in about two hours." That's about the time that it takes to tour the museum with a large group.

The Kids that were standing near the teacher started giving me high fives as they exited the streetcar. They were just doing what the teacher had done. Each member of this group of Passengers, including chaperons and teachers, gave me a high five before getting off of the streetcar. The high fives were cool, but; the little comments that the Kids were making was even better. I don't' know what motivates Kids to think of things, but; some of the comments that the Kids were making as they gave me a high five were cracking me up.

The last person of the group to get off of the streetcar was a chaperone. He looked at me and shook his head in disbelief. He said, "This group of Kids are usually quiet and reserved, I can't believe that they had so much fun just riding on the streetcar ride. "You know what?" he exclaimed, "I'm gonna bring my grandkids on this streetcar the next time that they come to visit us from Iowa. I want to see if they get excited too." As he turned to get off the streetcar he paused for a moment. He then turned toward me and gave me a high five. "Don't forget about us!" he said as he walked down the steps of the streetcar.

Using a Terminator phrase, I responded with my best Arnold voice, "I'll be back!" The chaperone just looked at me and shook his head. He got off of the streetcar and rejoined the group. As they headed toward the new museum, I resumed my route. It was still early in the day and I had a full day of driving in front of me. I drove back to the Transfer Center and there was nobody waiting at the streetcar stop, so; I drove on.

As I approached the bench where the guy was waiting for me; I wasn't sure how the guy was going to react after waiting for forty-five minutes or so. I was probably goin get chewed out by him for making him wait. Oh well, it wouldn't be the first time that it happened so I figured that I'd play it by ear and see what plays out. Sure enough, as I looked down the rails from my vantage point, I could see that the man was waiting for me to pick him up. As I neared him, he looked up at the streetcar, but; did not get up from the bench. I'm thinking that maybe he thought that I had more Kids on the streetcar or something.

I stopped the streetcar in front of him; opened the front door and bellowed, "All aboard." I thought of it as a way to kind of get him into the mood and break the ice.

He responded with, "Yea I coming. There aren't no Kids on there is there?

"Nope. I dropped all of them off at the new museum", I replied.

"Good! I can't be anywhere near Kids", he muttered back as he got up from the bench. "My probation officer said that he would send me back to prison if I don't behave myself. I really dislike that guy. You sure that there are no Kids on there, right?"

I'm thinking to myself, what have I gotten myself into? I answered with, "Nope, dropped them all off and the streetcar is empty.

The guy boarded the streetcar cautiously and was what I figured checking the streetcar out to make sure that there was no Kids on board. After he felt that it was clear of children; he sat down on the front seat to my right. "I'm going to the stop closest to the post office," he said as he settled in the seat.

"We'll be there shortly," I replied. After I checked my mirrors; I drove the streetcar down the tracks. As I approached the Post office the guy said to me. "How did you know that I wasn't supposed to be near Kids?"

I said to him, "I didn't know. The reason that I didn't let you on the streetcar with the Kids was because you have puke on the front of your shirt! Maybe you should go change your shirt because it's not cool to walk around like that. You know what I mean?"

"Yea, I know," he mumbled. "I got some problems that I'm trying to work out. Maybe I should go back home before I go to the Post Office, "He said to himself. We drove on.

As we neared the Post Office the guy said to me, "Hey change of plans, my man! Dropped me off where you picked me up so that I can go home and change."

"You got it," I immediately replied. I drove the streetcar down the line until I came to the bench that I had picked the guy up at. I pulled the streetcar to a stop and opened the front door so my lone Passenger could get off. I watched in the interior mirror as the man was getting up from his seat to exit the streetcar. As he walked to the exit-door he turned to me and said, "So you're telling me that the reason that you wouldn't let me ride the streetcar with those Kids was because I had dirty clothes on and not because you knew that I had problems with children?"

"Absolutely that was the reason! I know now that you have a problem with children because you told me that you do. I will definitely keep that in my mind the next time I see you. Let me make myself perfectly clear. I won't tell anybody about your problem, but: on the other hand, I won't hesitate to report you if I do see any problems. Are we on the same page?" was my stern reply.

"I understand," he muttered as he was exiting the streetcar. The only thing that I could think of as he walked away from the streetcar that day was that I hoped he could straighten himself out. I knew that he was going to go home and change his clothes, but; that was going to be the easy part. Changing his ways was going to be the hard part. I only hoped that I didn't give him any information that he could use to bother any children. I watched as the guy walked away from the streetcar.

That day when I ended my shift I wrote an incident report and turned it into my Dispatcher. On the report I stated what had happened and what the guy had told me. I wrote in detail what I had observed and hoped one of my superiors would act on it or even question my actions. I did it to cover my butt just incase the guy would want to make a big to do about me not letting him ride the streetcar, but: I also wanted to air my concerns about this guy.

For the next couple months I saw the guy hanging around the bus Transfer Center. He was cleaned up and well shaven. I never saw him bothering any of the Kids, but I kind of kept an eye on him because there was something about him that gave me a funny feeling. Some how I knew that I was going to have some kind of dealing with this guy in the future, although; I really hoped that I was going to be wrong. You know, there are some individuals that you just don't like. Well this guy was one of those individuals for me. I didn't trust him as far as I could throw him.

Then one day my fears came to life. While reading the local newspaper one morning I saw a picture of the man on the front page of the local news-paper. It seems that he had been involved in a Federal sting and was arrested for child pornography. The article stated that when he was arrested that thousands of photographs of young children were found in his possession. I was sick! Just to think that this guy was a predator of children, but; I knew that. I had some thoughts for him to myself that even today I feel ashamed for even thinking of them. I know that I'm a better person than that.

When you're a Bus Driver and deal with the public you have to keep reminding yourself that your job is to drive the bus. You have to keep telling yourself that you're not a social worker or psychologist. You have to learn to deal with the idea that whatever is going to happen, is going to happen. Even though you want to get involved in little incidents, you just can't. That is just part of the job.

Many times when incidents reports are written by Bus Drivers those reports, for whatever reason; are not acted upon or taken serious by those in charge. Yes, I do realize that people are to be presumed innocent until they are proven to be guilty, but; it's ridiculous the way many of those in charge won't take complaints seriously. I'm sure the ramifications of acting on some of these reports would put certain individuals in a bad light or even cause some extra paper work for someone. Tough luck!! Get over it and do your job to the best of your ability. Quite a few problems would go away and a whole lot of people would be better off if those in charge would think of others, rather; than being part of a good old boy system or a broken bureaucracy.

Chapter 25

Did you hit me with the Bus?

One bus route that I drive takes me from the downtown Transfer Center to the outskirts of our city. This route is specifically designed to get Passengers to and from work. The endpoint of this route is an intersection of two major highways. At this intersection there is a gathering of little outlet malls. It is one of those routes that are extremely important to those who use it because the jobs at these outlet malls are low paying and the worker are generally semi-skilled. The bus is the only inexpensive transportation that these individuals can rely on to get them to work on time. They probably could walk to work, but; the walk would be a long and dangerous one along a busy highway. It would not be practical and everybody knows it. If the workers would take a cab to work, the cost of the cab would take almost their entire daily wages so that option is usually not taken.

The timing of this bus route is dictated by traffic patterns. If the traffic is heavy, it takes a full fifteen to twenty minutes to go from the downtown Transfer Center to the midpoint of this route. If the traffic is light, it takes ten to twelve minutes to make the trip from the midpoint of the route to the Transfer Center. The midpoint of the route is at a shopping plaza where at certain times of the day the other bus routes converge.

One day while I was doing this route, I was fortunate enough to have light traffic patterns. As I drove toward the downtown area; I figured that I would get to the Transfer Center early. Getting there early would allow me to have a little extra time at the Transfer Center and take a well deserved break while I waited for the other buses to gather. I was right on my calculations and got downtown early. My assigned parking space for this route is out of the way and at the end of the Transfer Center. I have a very good view of Lake Michigan from this parking place because the lake shore is a few hundred yards away. As I parked the bus, I glanced at my watch and realized that I had about twelve minutes before the other buses were to arrive at the Transfer Center. Yippee; break time! This meant that I could finally eat that sandwich that I had not had the opportunity to eat earlier in the day.

I had one Passenger on my bus and we were just talking sports as I drank a hot cup of coffee from my thermos and was eating the aforementioned sandwich. As we sat there talking and waiting for the other buses to arrive, my lone Passenger said jokingly as he made a pointing gesture with his hand , "Hey Marty, look at this guy coming toward the bus. It looks like he can't walk a straight line."

I was seated in the Drivers' seat of the bus and looked in the direction that my Passenger was pointing. Keep in mind now that the bus has been parked in the same spot for at least five full minutes and my emergency flashers were on. When I'm parked at the Transfer Center I have my flashers on for safety reasons. My parking space at the Transfer Center has a lot of traffic, buses and cars, driving near my parked bus. I look at it as an extra safety precaution. As I looked out the front door bus window across the Transfer Center compound; I watched as a man walked toward my parked bus. At first glance, my first thought was that this person had either too much to drink or had some medical condition that impaired him from walking a straight line. The man that was walking toward the bus was staggering and walking slowly. I watched as he used the park benches, garbage cans and the bus shelters as so called points of reference. He was using these points of reference to steady himself and to prevent himself from falling over.

The conversation on the bus turned back to sports and the man walking toward the bus was for now a fleeting memory. I drank my coffee and listened to my lone Passenger tell me how good his favorite baseball team was going to be this year. Yea right! I was listening to my friend speak, but; I half heartedly kept an eye on the guy that was stumbling toward the bus. At that time I noticed that the other buses were starting to arrive at the Transfer Center. My bus now had been parked in the same spot for at least ten minutes.

The sports conversation was going on when a woman and a man boarded the bus and sat down. They were regulars who work out at the outlet mall and ride the bus daily. This was nothing out of the ordinary for either one of them. The woman went to the rear of the bus, while; the man, whom I always thought of as kind of weird, sat midway in the aisle. The man and woman did not sit together because they just got on the bus together, nothing more.

I finished my coffee and was putting my thermos away when the woman who had just boarded said, "Marty, look at this man walking toward the bus!" Everybody knows the Bus Drivers name. My attention, as well as everybody else's on the bus, immediately turned toward the man that was walking and stumbling toward the bus. We all sat there and watched as the man walked directly into the side of the bus. Walk would be the wrong word. Let's say he plowed face first into the side of the bus. He hit the bus so hard that the bus shook and it made a sounding thud. His face hit the bus about window high and everybody on the bus saw the look on the guys face when he made contact with the bus. It was like everything happening in slow motion. I really didn't believe my eyes! But it happened.

I jumped up from my seat and was heading out the bus door. I had the where with all to grab my hand radio in case I needed it. I got off the bus and rushed over to the man, who was now sitting on the ground next to the bus. As I got near the man, he looked up at me from his seated position. The man's face was covered in blood. He did not say a word. He was dazed. I immediately used my radio to contact Dispatch. I didn't use proper radio protocol; I just started talking into the radio. Needless to say, I was concerned and excited about the man's well being.

"I need an ambulance at the Transfer Center immediately," I said to my Dispatcher.

He responded with, "One is on the way. Another Driver saw the whole thing. Did the guy really walk into the side of the bus?"

"No, I would say he ran into the bus", I frantically responded.

I put my radio in my pocket and knelt down by the man who had gotten hurt. My intent was to keep him calm until the ambulance arrived. By now a crowd of people had gathered around my bus and many of them were making little comments that they saw the guy walk into the bus. I looked around at the faces, many of whom I knew, because I knew that I was going to have to write an incident report. They all were now my witnesses.

I gave the man on the ground a hanky and told him to put in on his forehead to stop the bleeding. He took the hanky and held it to his forehead. There was definitely a distinct smell of alcohol coming from the fellow. It wasn't a fruity smell so I immediately ruled out some kind of medical condition. What I smelled was the distinct odor of cheap booze. I told him that an ambulance was on the way. I stayed knelt by him to comfort him and give him reassurance.

I guess this was one of those days where you never know what's going happen next. The plot thickens. About that time the man that had walked into the side of the bus said to me. "Hey, you're a Bus Driver! Did you hit me with the bus? I'm going to sue you and the city; you 'Moron'!" He said enough for me. My compassion for the man ended right then and there. I stood up from my knelt position and said, "The ambulance is on its way, good luck my friend." He used up all Marty's compassion in one sentence. He was on his own as far as I was concerned.

I immediately walked to the front of the bus and took my radio out of my pocket. I calmly contacted Dispatch again and told them that they might want to send a Police officer down to the Transfer Center because the guy was drunk. At that time I also relayed to Dispatch what the man had told me about suing the city and calling me a Moron.

"Marty, you have at least five other Drivers who saw what happened. Don't worry. Make sure you write an incident report and get plenty of witness names," Dispatch responded.

I replied, "10-4. Thanks"

I got back on the bus and was going through my paper work looking for an incident report. I looked out my windshield and the ambulance was pulling up. The crowd that was gathered around the man on the ground was alerting the ambulance to where the man on the ground was. No need for me to get off the bus and waste my time. I found an incident report and started filling it out. I figure to get some witness names before the crowd broke up. It then dawned on me that I had three Passengers on the bus that witnessed the incident. That would be more than enough witnesses. I said to my three Passengers, "Could I please use you guys as witnesses? I just want you to say that you saw the guy walk into the side of the bus and that the bus was parked. Just the truth, that's all."

My friend, the man that I was talking sports to said, "No problem Marty! Give me a piece of paper and a pen I'll do it right now."

The lady who was seated at the back of the bus said," Absolutely! This is the most exciting thing that happened all week!"

But, the respond from the man who was seated on the bus was completely different. He looked at me with a very stoic face and sternly said, "I didn't see nothing! I don't witness nothing for nobody. Do you understand me? Just leave me alone and don't bother me."

His reaction to my request was a surprise to me and took me completely off guard. Trying to be a professional, I said, "Thanks to each of you and if you chose not to witness; I fully understand." What I really wanted to say and what I said were two different things. I just don't understand how some people think. Whatever!

The ambulance was now gone and all the excitement was over. The other buses that were at the Transfer Center had already left or were in the process of leaving. I needed to get going on my route because now I was running behind schedule. As I drove out to the midpoint of my route nobody on the bus spoke a word. I thought that it was kind of funny, but; I really didn't put much, more thought into it. I was thinking to myself as I drove the route that I hoped the guy that was drunk didn't get hurt too bad. I'm a soft touch I guess.

When I got to the midpoint of the route the man and woman got off and went to another bus. My friend stayed on the bus. Nobody else got on or was coming toward the bus so I resumed my route.

As we drove on my friend said to me, "What was that guy's problem?"

I assumed that he was talking about the guy that walked into the bus so I answered with. "Awe he was just drunk."

"Not the Drunk! I'm talking bout, Mister I don't see Nothin," my friend sarcastically replied.

"Some people are just like that. They don't want to help anyone, but; if they ever need help or something they're the first to ask for it. I wouldn't worry about it," I replied. We drove on.

I dropped my friend off at the end of my route and he went to work. I continued on with my route and eventually ended up back down town parked at the Transit Center. I thought about the things that happened earlier in the day and something funny struck me. It dawned on me that if the bus wouldn't have been parked there and if the drunken individual had kept walking; would he have stopped before he came to the lake or would he have fallen into the lake. Remember I told you that Lake Michigan is only few hundred yards from where the buses park. I think that the only thing that kept him from falling in the lake that day was the bus. I really don't know, but; I think of it as the bus saving his life. I'm sure that the drunken man doesn't think of things that way. I'm sure that in his mind that he is convinced that I'm a "Moron" and that I hit him with the bus that day.

Chapter 26

TRANSIT GUMSHOES'

When Bus Drivers are at the Transfer Center waiting for all the other buses to arrive; they see individuals doing all sorts of activities. Most of these activities are just human nature and we as humans think nothing wrong of doing them. These little things that people do usually satisfy and itch or relieve the body of some type of discomfort. You know things like: scratching places on their body; or just talking to themselves. Everybody does it! People must think that the Bus Drivers don't notice little things like that, but; we do. Our profession is one that is based on observations. We need to know our surrounding in order to execute our job safely. So overall I would say that Bus Drivers are very observant and aware of their surroundings.

One morning when I was parked at the Transfer Center; I witness a young man selling what I thought to be "Drugs" to the other students. The kid didn't look like a Drug Dealer. You know the kind of person that I'm talking about; I'm talking about the kind of person that we all picture in our minds as a kind of low life who sells drugs. We all have our own ideas on what a Drug Dealer looks like, but; I'm telling you that this suspected Drug Dealer looked like and was an ordinary Junior High School Student.

This kid was very aware of his surroundings and acted as if he had complete control of all of his actions. He seemed to be very popular with quite a few of the other students, but; never spoke to them. That was weird. What brought this kid to my attention was his kinesics. His body language gave me the impression that he was doing something wrong. He was acting cool and nonchalant, but yet; he was looking around and acting sneaky.

Here is what would happen. Kids would come up to this Sneaky Kid and without saying a word give him money. Is that suspicious or not? The Sneaky Kid in turn would put the money into his courier like back pack and give the kid that gave him the money a small plastic bag. The kid would take the plastic bag and just walk away from the Sneaky Kid without saying a word. The Sneaky Kid always kept the courier backpack on his shoulder and safeguarded it in front of him. He never said a word to the other Kids; he always just nodded his head or waved his hand. I witnessed transactions like this numerous times.

After a couple times of seeing these little transactions, I decided that enough was enough. I called my Dispatcher and told them what I had seen. I had students seated on my bus and students getting on my bus, so; when I was speaking to my Dispatcher, I was speaking softly so the students couldn't hear my conversation. I told Dispatch about the kid's coming up to the Sneaky Kid and giving him money. I also told Dispatch how the Sneaky Kid in turn would give the Kids a small plastic bag. After giving all the information to the Dispatcher that I possibly could; I said to the Dispatcher, "Do yaw think that we can get something done about this?"

Dispatch responded with, "How do you know that the Sneaky Kid ain't selling cookies to the other Kids?"

I said, "What? Did you hear anything that I told you?"

Dispatch responded with, "Yes I did! I asked you, how do you know that the Sneaky Kid ain't selling cookies to the other Kids?"

I humbly and inquisitively replied, "I don't! What does cookies got to do with this?'

"We can't jump to conclusions", Dispatch firmly answered back. Write an incident report and turn it in today and I'll talk to those in charge. 10-4?"

"10-4", I reluctantly replied. I got the feeling that I had just been blown off.

It was time to leave the Transfer Center and continue my route. All the other buses that were at the Transfer Center were starting to pull out of their parking spaces to carry on with their respected duties. The Transfer Center was now deserted of Kids. All the Kids that were milling around the Transfer Center were now on the buses and would be headed toward the schools throughout the city. I tried to keep track of which transit bus that the Sneaky Kid had gotten on, but; there were just way too many Kids moving around for me to keep track of. I was also trying to do quite a few things at one time and probably shouldn't have been talking on the phone to Dispatch in the first place. You know things like taking bus transfers; making sure that the Kids put the right amount of money into the fare-box and generally keeping order on my bus.

I drove my transit route that day and didn't have any other out of the ordinary incidents happen. I was thankful for that. At the end of the shift, at the transit garage, I wrote a well detailed incident report of what had transpired that morning at the Transfer Center. In the incident report I explained why and what my concerns were. I aired my suspicions and wanted to know what could be done to prevent these activities from occurring at the Transfer Center. No where in that incident report did I use the word "cookies." I went home that night with a sour taste in my mouth because somehow I knew that this problem wouldn't be handled properly.

The next morning when I arrived at the Transfer Center and drove my bus into my assigned parking spot, I couldn't believe my eyes of what I was seeing. Leaning on the park bench, the same one that I had detailed in my incident report the evening before was one of the Transit garage mechanics. It was obvious that he was a city employee by the clothes that he was wearing. He was leaning on the park bench with his one foot on the seat and resting his butt on the park bench backrest and acting like a big shot. In his right hand was a hand held radio that he was holding to his face and talking into. I have no idea who he was talking to. As he was talking into the radio; he was looking around at all the nearby students and giving them the impression that he was looking for something or someone. Better yet, standing about ten feet away from the Super Sleuth Mechanic was one of the Transit Supervisors dressed in a business suit. He too, was holding a hand held radio and talking into it. As I watched from the bus; I came to the conclusion that they were talking to each other on the radio. I think that I stumbled upon a secret covet operation. There was a group of students waiting to board my bus as I pulled up and the Mechanic and the Supervisor were keeping a close eye on them.

The Kids on the other hand were keeping a watchful eye on the two Super Sleuths.

My first thought was that Dick Tracy and Barney Fife were on the case. I parked my bus, opened the front door and got off. As soon as I parked the bus, students started to board. I couldn't walk away from the bus and leave it unattended with students onboard, so I stood outside the bus by the front door. I could hear the radio conversation that the Mechanic and the Supervisor was having from at least ten feet away from them. As the students boarded the bus, some of them were making comments about the two guys with radios. The one student was telling the other student that the guy by the park bench asked him if he was selling Mary Jane or something like that. The student said that he looked at the guy and just walked away laughing. Another kid said that he thought that the two guys with the radios were CSI agents because it looked like something that he saw on TV the night before.

The Mechanic and the Supervisor watched me as I stood by the bus door. You could tell that they wanted to talk to me, so; in a normal voice I said, "Good morning. What's up?"

They both walked over to me as I stood by the bus. The supervisor said to me, "Did you see that kid that was supposedly selling drugs down here?"

"No I didn't, but; I'll keep my eyes open and let you know immediately if I see anything going down," I sarcastically replied. The mechanic didn't say a word; he just shook his head in agreement with what I had said. When he did that it reminded me of Barney Fife. I was waiting for him to reach into his front shirt pocket and produce his lone silver bullet to show me. He didn't, but; I'm sure he was thinking about it. After I thought about it for a second I realized that he couldn't have because he did have a radio in his hand. I must of had a smirk on my face because both the Supervisor and the Mechanic gave me a dirty look. I said to myself, "Whatever! Have a nice day guys." I then turned and walked back onto my bus.

The buses started to pull out of their spaces and it was time to go on our routes. I got on the bus and announced to my Passengers that we were leaving and they all took their seat. I was one of the last buses to leave the Transfer Center. As I was pulling out of the Transfer Center;

I watched as the Supervisor and the Mechanic resumed their vigil of standing by the park bench and looking for drug dealers. What a joke! I knew that they would mess it up. For the rest of the morning the two Super Sleuths held their ground by the park bench. What a waste of taxpayer money I thought.

The rest of the day went pretty good and there were no issues that came up. Even in the afternoon after school, when all the students were at the Transfer Center, it was quiet. After all, word spread really fast amongst the students that there were two city employees with radios looking for drug dealers. Some of the other Drivers were making little comments about what had happened that day at the Transfer Center. Word spread like wild fire that Transit personnel was trying to catch drug dealers now as part of their job. Everybody thought it was funny the way the situation was being handled. That was everybody, except me. I wanted that Sneaky Kid to stop selling whatever it was to other Kids. That night I went home extremely frustrated and disappointed with my dim-witted Superiors.

A couple days went by and all was quiet at the Transfer Center. I didn't observe any selling of whatever at the Transfer Center and I was happy. On the forth day business for the Sneaky Kid started up again, after all; there weren't any guys with radios glued to their faces hanging around. That morning the Sneaky Kid was back in business. I watched as he was selling bags of whatever to the other Kids. I immediately contacted my Dispatcher and told them that the Sneaky Kid was selling things to the other Kids again. Dispatch told me that he would tell my superiors and I was not to approach the kid. It wasn't my job to confront the Sneaky Kid, so I had no plans to.

Time came for the buses to leave the Transfer Center and all the Kids that were at the Transfer Center ran to their perspective buses. Again I couldn't keep track of what bus that the Sneaky Kid had gotten on because of all the other Kids milling around. He did his selling again and got away with it. I was very aggravated. I just hoped that nobody gets sick from whatever he was selling. After all the students were on my bus and settled down; I resumed my route.

Later that morning my Superior contacted me through my radio and said that he wanted to talk to me when I got back to the garage that evening. I told him that after I post tripped my bus that I would gladly meet him in his office. The rest of the day went by rather slowly because of my anxiety and anticipation of what the upcoming meeting with my Superior would bring. The day finally ended and it was time to meet with my Boss. I walked up to his office door and knocked on it. My Supervisor, in a very bold voice, told me to come in and grab a seat. I sat down in the big comfy chair directly in front of his paper cluttered desk. His desk was cluttered with lottery tickets and sports pools. After all he was responsible for the office pools for: the Parks department; The Water department; The Waste department; and The Transit Department. If there was an office pool going round he was the one who started it. I knew by the way that he was acting; that I was going to get chewed out for something. Sure enough!

My supervisor said to me, "We investigated your claim of students selling drugs at the Transfer Center downtown and didn't find any evidence of it. You need to stop bothering Dispatch and just do your job. Your job is to drive the bus, that's all. Do I make myself perfectly clear?"

What choices did I have? I knew better than to start arguing with him about my claims because the way he was acting was that he already had his mind made up and there would be no changing of it. Not wanting to continue with this charade, I felt that it was time to leave. So I stood up from my seated position and I humbly replied, "No problem. Have a good evening." I then proceeded to exit his office and headed for the locker room.

As I was leaving my Supervisor said, "Thanks for stopping. By the way, you're doing a good job out there." It's something that he always says whether he means it or not. It's just his empathetic way of trying to build teamwork and camaraderie amongst the employees. All the other Drivers know this and just play along with Management's little mind games. Nobody really buys into it. When I left the Transit garage that night I knew that the Transit Management had washed their hands of the problem and nothing was going to be done about it. Typical! After all, why should they have to carry the burden; it's not their job.

After I got home that night, I made a phone call to a Police Officer that I know quite well. I told them who I was, but; this call was to be considered anonymous. I reminded my friend that I was a City Transit

Driver and then relayed the story of what has been happening at the Transfer Center. I went into great detail about the Sneaky Kid and his exploits. Any detail that I could remember about the Sneaky Kid, I told my friend. You know the park bench he hangs out at; the satchel bag; his Modus operandi; and any other detail I could think of. I also told the Police Officer of how I tried to go through the proper channels to get this matter resolved, but; my concerns fell upon the deaf ears of my Superiors. I told my friend that Transit Officials just didn't want to get involved. I made it very clear of how my job would possibly be in jeopardy if Transit Officials found out about this phone call, so; it would be greatly appreciated if he could use this information with the utmost confidentiality.

The Police officer, my friend, said in a very professional voice, "We'll see yaw at the bowling alley Wednesday night and Thank you sir. We'll take care of that little problem for you." When he hung up the phone, I knew that the problem was going to be taken care of, but; I didn't know when or how. I really didn't want to make that phone call, but; I felt that I was obligated to. I was obligated not only to myself, but; to the general public. Just because I'm a Bus Driver doesn't mean that I can't do things as a Taxpaying Concerned Citizen. I know that I did the right thing even though if my superior's found out that they would not condone it. I don't care because I have grandchildren, nieces, nephews and numerous student friends who use the Transit System bus and I am not taking any chances with their well being. I went to bed that night with a good feeling of what was going to happen.

I got to work the next morning and didn't tell any of the other Drivers about the phone call that I had made the night before. I figured that I would just wait and see what happens. As I drove the bus to the Transfer Center to start my route; I thought of it as one day closer to my retirement. Please don't insult my intelligence and say that you have never done that. Everybody does it at one time or another, so don't act like you don't. It's something that gives us all some kind of fleeting hope. OK!

All the students were starting to assemble at the Transfer Center when I arrived at my bus's assigned parking spot. I was keeping an eye out for the Sneaky Kid. From my vantage point, the Driver's seat of the bus, but nothing looked out of the ordinary at the Transfer Center. It was just another day in Paradise.

After I was parked for about five minutes or so I watched as the Sneaky Kid showed up and walked up to his normal park bench and started looking around. Yep, he was looking for customers. After about a minute or two I watched as another student walked up to the Sneaky Kid. The student then looked around as if she too was trying not to be noticed and then, in a sly manner, she gave the Sneaky Kid some money. The Sneaky Kid took the money and put it into his pants pocket. The Sneaky Kid then reached into the satchel bag that he was carrying and gave the other student a small plastic bag of something. The student that had given him the money took the plastic bag from him, looked around and started to walk away with their purchased goods. I was thinking about now; here we go again. Boy was I wrong!

Four Police officers appeared out of nowhere. All the officers were dressed in plain clothes and fit into the crowd perfectly. Two of the officers approached the Sneaky Kid and the other two officers approached the student with the small plastic bag. I said to myself, "Busted!"

The look on the Sneaky Kid's face was priceless. He too knew that his selling days were over. I think that for a second that he thought about running. He obviously knew that he had no where to go. Besides, what could he do? He had two broad-shouldered Police Officers standing next to him with his arms being held by each of them. In one swift move; the Police officers had the Sneaky Kid handcuffed and under control. His satchel bag was now being held by one of the Officers.

The student that had purchased the bag of whatever was now also handcuffed and was being led to an unmarked Police car that appeared out of nowhere. The entire incident was over in less than two minutes. What I thought was great was that quite a few of the other students saw what had happened. It's kind of funny, but; Kids have an unwritten code. If they know something about something illegal going on; they won't say anything about it because they don't want to get involved or are afraid to say something. It's not that they condone it; it's that they don't know how to confront it without really getting involved. You know peer pressure. On the other hand, if something happens where the problem gets solved, like in the manner that this was, the Kids will openly talk about it. It's funny how that works. I think that it's kind of a defense mechanism or something that the kid's have. I'm sure that some well-educated individual has done or will do some kind of study on this now just to prove me wrong, but; whatever?

The rest of the day went by pretty fast. Word spread quickly about the incident that had happen that morning at the Transfer Center. Why wouldn't it? After all many of the Bus Drivers saw what happened and they mentioned it to their Passengers all day; the students that saw it, mentioned to all their friends at the various schools around the city and it snowballed from there. By that afternoon everybody and anybody that has anything to do with riding or driving the bus knew about it. I though that it was a real good deterrent for future sellers.

A couple days went by and everything was back to normal, minus the Sneaky Kid's activities, at the Transfer Center. The activities at the Transfer Center had changed and life went on. The only thing constant was the buses coming and going. What happened yesterday and the day before were now memories and in the past. About a week after the incident concerning the Sneaky Kid, I received a radio call from my Superior requesting that I stop in his office when I completed my shift. He had some questions that he wanted to ask me. I told him that after I completed my Post-trip that day that I would stop by his office. I knew exactly what he wanted to talk about.

The day went by quickly and before I knew it I was knocking on my Superior's office door at the end of my shift. My Superior bellowed out for me to come in and grab a seat. See some things never change. I walked into the room and sat down in the big comfy chair in front of my Boss's paper cluttered desk. My boss got up from his desk and walked over and closed the office door. He was rather somber. He walked back to his desk and sat down. He cleared his throat and made a sigh to himself before he made eye contact with me. I could tell that he didn't want to have this conversation. Kinesics told the whole story. The conversation started out with him saying, "So have you seen anymore drug activities at the Transfer Center?"

I replied with, "No sir. You told me not to bother you guys with that stuff and that my job was to just drive the bus."

"Good!" My boss smugly replied. I just wanted to let you know that I contacted the Police Department this morning about your concerns and they told me that that issue has been resolved.

I said in a surprised voice, "You mean the problem has been solved?"

"Absolutely, we took care of that predicament! I was going to do a little bit more investigating on this matter, but; since I was officially told that the problem was solved, I consider this a non-issue from here on. Thanks for stopping by and by the way keep up the good work out there." he pompously said.

I got up from the big comfy chair and started to walk toward the door. As I was leaving his office to go home I turned to my superior and said, "Thank you sir and have a good evening." I couldn't say what I wanted to say because it surely would have cost me my job. Later that evening as I lay in my bed trying to go to sleep; I thought of how secure I should feel at work knowing that Dick Tracy and Barney Fife were on the job watching over me and my brethren Bus Drivers. I also had a thought of wondering how the office pool lottery numbers had fared that evening in the drawing, not that I participated, but; it quickly dawned on me that that too was a non-issue because the pool was in the competent hands of my Superiors. But then again what do I know? I just drive the bus.

Chapter 27

THE ENVELOPE

It's good to know that our actions can really make a difference in another person's life. First impressions last a life time and it's said that you never get the opportunity for that first time again. I for one don't believe that. In my first book I told you two stories about the guy in the "Little red sports-car". You know just from reading these stories that I told you; what kind a guy he truly is. Not once; but twice he let his true colors fly. Remember the circular drive at the hospital when he left his briefcase on the roof of his little red car? Or perhaps you remember his little escapade at the gas station when he was running through standing traffic and swearing at the other motorists while he was looking for that elusive twenty dollar bill.

His actions in both of these anecdotes gave us all the impressions of a spoiled rotten, self centered, egotistical, vulgar individual. Those are insensitive word coming out of me, but; at the time they fit. This individual really gave us all a lasting first and second impression, didn't he? Awe, maybe I was a little harsh, but; I callem like I see em. I'm thinking that these impressions are just illusions of what that individual wants others to see. After reconsidering everything that I've seen, I would say that this individual is in fact, the exact opposite of the image that he is personifying. It's said that a leopard can't change its spots. I'm wondering if all along I was looking at the wrong spots on this leopard. To be fair, I must tell you this; there is a third story about this individual that I would be remiss if I didn't tell you.

A while back there was a tragic event in our community where children were involved. The talk on the bus for quite a few days centered on the innocent victims, the children. I'm not going to go into any details about the mishap because the matter is in litigation and I don't want to assume the responsibility of perhaps messing up some sort of appeal process, so; I'll just leave you with this thought on the subject. Children are innocent and each and every one of them deserves a fighting chance. When children are used as pawns and disposable objects, the outcome is never good. If their parents are Loser's and drag the Kids into situations where the outcome will inevitably become violent, then others need to intervene. That intervention can come in a variety of actions. Whatever action is taken I hope that the children's well being is considered first.

Like I said, everyone was talking about "should of been" and "could have beens" on this incident. I felt that it was just too bad that these thoughts didn't come up sooner. There were numerous financial institutions in our community that set up trust funds for this family to help them through this ordeal. My wife and I decide that we needed to get involved even though it was after the fact. We decided that we should give a monetary donation and maybe in some way it would help with the healing process that the family was going through. Obviously we weren't the only ones with that thought, as I soon found out.

After driving my shift on the Transit Bus all day, I stopped at one of the local financial institutions that were championing the collecting cause. I drove to the bank that day with a heart full of guilt and a pocket full of cash. I guess that I'm exaggerating about a pocketful of cash. In reality it was just a check with a small amount written on it, but; the thought was there. I usually wear my heart on my sleeve and I'm sure that today it was showing. The amount of check itself was not a lot, but; it was what my wife and I figured that we could afford.

I parked my personal car and started to walk toward the bank. As I walked through the parking lot toward the bank entrance, I noticed a little red sports car pulling into a handicap parking space in front of the bank. I immediately recognized the little red car as the one that I had had encounters with in the past. I instinctively glanced at the license plate of the car to see if there was a handicap plate. There wasn't. I then looked into the windshield and there was no handicap stickers present there either. What a jerk I thought as I walked into the bank lobby.

When I got through the bank doors and entered the bank lobby; I looked around the lobby for where the Tellers windows were located.

As I was walking up to one of the Teller's windows, the Teller asked me if I was there to make a donation and she then mentioned the family's name. I told her "Yes I was." The Bank Teller then directed me with her hand in a sweeping motion toward a line of people standing in front of a bank representative's office. I thanked her as I walked toward the line of people.

There were perhaps ten people standing in line and I took my place at the end of the line. By some of the comments that the people in the line made as I walked up to the line; I could tell that the line was moving slowly. From my place at the end of the line, I leaned over and looked toward the front of the line toward the Bank Representative's office. In the office sat the Bank Rep behind his desk and in the chair in front of the Banker's desk sat a man talking to the Banker. It was obvious after a few seconds that they were just socializing. It wasn't my place to complain, after all; no one had drug me into the bank and forced me to stand in that line. That doesn't mean that my wife had nothing to do with me being there, but; I probably shouldn't go there either, if you know what I mean.

As I stood in line waiting, I was leaning on one of those kiosk islands that all the banks have strategically located throughout their lobbies. You know those little podiums that I'm talking about; the ones with pens, deposit slips and a little slot that serves as a garbage can attached to them. Well anyways, as I stood there waiting, guess who should come walking up to the same kiosk as me? Yep, it was the guy from the little red car. I recognized him immediately, but; I'm sure that he hadn't a clue who I was. Heck, I was dressed in my Transit uniform; you figure that that would be a dead giveaway, but it wasn't.

The fellow walked up to me as I stood by the kiosk and he very politely asked," Excuse me Sir, is this line where we can contribute to that family?"

I replied to him with, "Yes and the line isn't moving." He sighed and took a step toward me. He was now standing behind me. In doing so, the guy had now taken his place as the guy at the end of a line that wasn't moving.

I watched as the guy glanced at his watch and then took his wallet out and placed it on the podium. He seemed to be in a hurry or late for something. I figured it as a guy thing, you know; us guys don't like to stand in lines. We always got important things to do and ain't got time for standing in stupid lines. Anyways, he then proceeded to take seven crisp one hundred dollars bills out of his wallet and insert them into one of the envelopes that were available on the kiosk. He then sealed the envelope and picked up the kiosk pen. He proceeded to blot out some of the writings that had been stamped on the envelope. He then, in very bold block letters, wrote the name of the family that the contribution was for and signed it with "From Anonymous".

I was dumbfounded. Is this the same guy that I had experienced in the past? I said to myself, "Mind your own business." OK, so I stood in line looking forward acting as if I hadn't seen a thing.

That's when the guy said to me, "Excuse me, but; don't I know you? You look familiar and I can't place where I know you from. Do you bowl?"

"Yea I do", I shot back at him. I figured don't make waves. You know?

He looked at me and very seriously said, "Say could you do me a big favor?"

I was taken aback and replied with, "Yea I guess. What's up?"

He very humbly started with, "A couple years back my wife and I lost our only child through very much the same circumstances as this family did. It was a little different, but; the out come was the same. We know what their going though. Well anyways, my wife and I want to make a contribution to this family and I have an important meeting that I need to go to, so; could you turn this envelope in for me. I'd really appreciate if you could do that for us."

Well I figured that I was standing in line anyways, so: why not! "No problem! I can do that for you," I respectfully replied.

"Great! Thanks a lot Sir; I really appreciate it! I owe you!" he said. With that, he handed me the envelope that I had watch him prepare. After giving me the envelope; he turned and started walking through the lobby toward the front door of the bank. As he was opening the door; he turned back toward me and waved. I stood there in line and watched as he exited the bank and got into his little red sports car.

The front window of the bank gave me a clear view of the parking lot. I watched as the little red sports car rapidly backed out of the handicap parking spot and almost collide with a delivery truck. The Driver of the little red sports car, obviously mad at the near collision with the delivery truck, stuck his head and arm out of the sports car window and verbally assaulted the delivery truck Driver. I couldn't hear what was being said, but; I knew that an argument was in process. I was astonished as I watched as the driver of the red sports car give the delivery truck Driver the "One fingered salute" and then drive away.

I must tell you that I was totally confused. I was wondering if I had met Doctor Jekyll and Mister Hyde. No really it happened that fast. I'm thinking that that little red sports-car was possessed and that it had a Svengallie affect on its Driver. I stood in line wondering if I needed to go wash my hands or something so that I didn't catch what he had. Then the thought came to me that if I go wash my hands, then I'll lose my place in line and have to be here longer. I was now the last one in line again, so; I just stood in line looking forward and thinking about what I had just witnessed. I glanced at the envelope that the guy had given me and wondered if I should drop it or kind of intentionally lose it, but; that wasn't going to happen. It was now my responsibility and I intended to complete my mission.

I stood in line for the next twenty or so mind-numbing minutes. I was the last person standing in the line for the entire twenty or so minutes. Every couple minutes or so; the line would move toward the Bank Representatives office. Everybody standing in line would half step forward as if we were all shackled together at the ankles as if we were prisoners or something. Us people standing in line could tell the regular bank customers from the visitors by the way the Bank Representative greeted us as we got to the front of the line. If you were a Regular Bank Customer, the Bank Representative invited you into his office for a little chat. Before these people left the office they were given calendars, pens and other little trinkets. On the other hand, if you weren't a Regular Bank Customer, the business at hand was handled while you stood in front of the Bank Representative's office. No trinkets for you! I thought of it as a poor way to do business, but; that's the way banks treat most people and most of us are use to it. I think its called cronyism.

When I finally got to the front of the line and it was my turn to take care of business, the Bank Representative came out of his office and said to me, "I'll be right with you, I have to see this man standing over here." And then and started to walk away.

I immediately responded with, "Well then I'll just grab a seat in your office and help myself to some of those calendars and candies that you were giving out to the other people that were in your office. Thanks" I then proceeded to start to walk into his office. I never made it that far.

The Bank Representative immediately stopped and turned toward me. In a frustrated voice he said, "How can I help you?"

I said, "I have these two envelopes that I wanted to drop off for that fund raiser that you're bank is having for that family. One of the envelopes is from the one guy who had to leave and the other one is from my wife and me."

With that being said, the Bank Representative reached out his grubby little hand and took the envelopes from me. He walked into his office and threw the envelopes on his desk. He then exited his office and closed the door. As he walked away from me he said, "Thank you, Have a nice day."

"Yea, you too Pal! But before you run off, don't I get a receipt or something?" Without saying a word, the anxious Bank Officer went back into his office, opened his desk drawer and took out some paper forms. He then walked back to me and hesitantly gave the two paper forms to me. "Fill these out. You can us these for tax purpose," he smugly said.

I took the forms from him and didn't say a word. I chuckled as I walked toward the bank door to get to my car. I couldn't get out of there fast enough. My mind was going a mile a minute as I walked out of the bank. My first thought was "I sure glad that I don't do my banking here" and my second thought was about the guy that drives the little red car. They both made lasting first impression on me. The guy with the little red car, well; I'm sure that in the future I'll have other dealing with him. But with him, I kind of know what to expect. On the other hand I'm almost absolutely positive that I won't be dealing with that Bank Representative again. That is of course if I got anything to say about it. But, that too depends on what my wife decides what we should do. Hey, what do I know? I just drive the bus.

Well the book is over and I want to tie up one loose end. My friend, in Chapter Four, will never see her hundred and first birthday because she is now resting and with her husband.

Thanks for reading my books and Yaw all be careful out there. I'm out of here for now. Later!!!

CPSIA information can be obtained at www.ICGtesting.com
Printed in the USA
LVOW090601151011

250652LV00001B/57/P